Access to
History

Other titles in the series:

Access to Citizenship

Access to Science

Access to History

Curriculum planning and practical activities for pupils with learning difficulties

Andrew Turner

David Fulton Publishers

London

David Fulton Publishers Ltd
Ormond House, 26–27 Boswell Street, London WC1N 3JZ

www.fultonpublishers.co.uk

First published in Great Britain in 2002 by David Fulton Publishers

Note: The right of Andrew Turner to be identified as the author of this work has been asserted by him in accordance with the Copyright, Designs and Patents Act 1988.

British Library Cataloguing in Publication Data
A catalogue record for this book is available from the British Library.

ISBN 1–85346–857–6 ✓

Typeset by FiSH Books, London
Printed in Great Britain by Bell & Bain Ltd, Glasgow

Contents

To my family
My own past, present, future

Introduction

History is the witness that testifies to the passing of time; it illumines reality, vitalises memory, provides guidance in daily life and brings us tidings of antiquity.

Marcus Tullius Cicero 106–43 BC

To have a new vision of the future, it has always first been necessary to have a new vision of the past.

Theodore Zeldin 1995

We are all products of our pasts, and the past is always with us, carried in innumerable ways – the way we speak, the colour of our eyes, the stories we know, the stories we tell. We need this baggage. Without a sense of history, both personal and social, we would be adrift. Knowledge of a wider past helps us to make sense of the world we live in. Knowledge of our own past gives us an important measure of ourselves. Much of how we define ourselves is made up of our experiences and by our relationships as they develop over time. We are creatures of our times and of times past.

Because of this, history fascinates us. Interest in the past has never been greater. In many senses the past has never been so present in our lives. On television, in books, on the Internet; the past is everywhere. One of the biggest uses of the Internet is for researching family history. Genealogy is big business. A quick glance at the television listings reveals a multitude of programmes about the history of famous and ordinary people, from the earliest times to the most recent.

The teaching of history in schools has also aroused comment and interest in recent years, although much of the debate has centred around what sort of history should be delivered to mainstream pupils. However, despite all of this, the issues around the teaching of history to pupils with special educational needs has been relatively unexplored, albeit with some notable exceptions.

There will be many reasons for this; the pressure on teachers to introduce a subject based curriculum to pupils who until very recently have been taught in other ways, the importance of the 'core subjects' of English, maths, science, and the doubt in the minds of some practitioners that history is somehow too abstract, too complex, or both for many of their pupils to grasp.

This book attempts to explore some of those issues around the teaching of history to pupils with learning difficulties. I explain why history is important for this group of pupils (and this is essentially for the same reasons it's important for any of us). I also demonstrate that history can be approached in a number of ways which allow teachers to develop meaningful work with a wide range of pupils. In addition, I advocate a way of thinking about history which is essentially inclusive. It can be redefined as a subject in a way which makes the teaching of it possible to all pupils. My view is that history can be seen as a unique set of stories about the lives of others, a way of apprehending what I have called 'the otherness of the past' and a means by which pupils can be encouraged to develop a sense of themselves as individuals with unique pasts. All of these things matter, and all offer a way of further enriching the lives of pupils. We can work towards giving all of them a new vision of the past, and through that, a new vision of their own present and of their possible futures.

CHAPTER ONE

Why history for pupils with learning difficulties?

History? You must be joking. You are joking, aren't you? Tell me you are.

A teacher of pupils with severe learning difficulties, circa 1988

Teaching the history of other people

The teaching of history has always been a contentious issue among teachers of pupils with learning difficulties. Anecdotal evidence suggests that it has often been seen as one of the most difficult subjects to make accessible to pupils with special needs and the greater the degree of learning difficulty, the greater the anxiety over how history could be delivered. Some practitioners may have also questioned whether or not there was any clear reason why it should be delivered. The debate over the relevance of the National Curriculum for some pupils has usually included a reference to History as an example of a 'subject too far'. For schools and individuals struggling to come to grips with the cultural changes brought about by the 1988 Education Reform Act, history teaching has been seen as, at the very least, a challenge.

However, to place the debate over history teaching and pupils with special educational needs in its own historical context we need to look at the views which first began to emerge in relation to pupils with moderate learning difficulties (or slow learners as they were then known) in the 1970s. At that time, a number of writers set out to challenge the assumption that such pupils could not or should not have access to a history curriculum. These writers made significant claims for the teaching of history which went beyond the acquisition of particular subject knowledge and often concentrated upon the skills and attitudes such study could develop, for example:

- increased critical abilities;
- an understanding of society;
- developing an increased tolerance of other groups, through an understanding of their historical contexts;
- instilling an awareness of change;
- extending the breadth of pupils' experiences to include work on local and national history
  (Cowie 1979)

- providing a catalyst for reflection on the present
  (Birt 1976)

- broadening children's educational experiences and widening their horizons (Galletley 1981)

- providing the more able pupils with a greater awareness of their own existence and providing the least able with a curriculum which is enriched by historical studies, and which provides contexts for the development of other skills (Martin and Gummet 1996).

In addition to the above, perhaps one of the most interesting contributions to thinking about the role of history and pupils with learning difficulties came from Roberts (1972). Roberts argued that history should be seen as an art, and therefore open to many levels of understanding. This was a way of thinking which could have led to some radical redefinitions of what history teaching and learning might look like for pupils with a range of learning difficulties. However, the idea does not seem to have been taken up by any other writer in the field of history and special needs. Nevertheless, a very similar line of thought emerged some 27 years later in the writings of Grove (1998), whose work on literature and pupils with learning difficulties offers some very useful insights into a potentially inclusive way of teaching history to pupils with a range of learning difficulties.

In her work, Grove argues that there is a continuum from apprehension and comprehension in the way stories are understood, and this continuum allows us to talk meaningfully about an inclusive approach to teaching literature.

> The reinstatement of feeling and sensation as the basis of response to literature changes how we think about the understanding of texts, in ways which are extremely helpful when we consider the difficulties faced in decoding complex language by students with special educational needs. It means that we need to make a distinction between *apprehension* and *comprehension*. (Grove 1998)

The same approach can arguably be taken with the subject of history. Such a view makes possible a definition of 'doing history' which starts from an affective response to aspects of the past. However, before I attempt to redefine what might count as 'doing history' in terms of teaching pupils with special needs, it is perhaps useful to remember that many historians have always accepted that historical understanding is not an either/or state. The very nature of history has always forced historians to acknowledge their partial and conditional understanding of it. For example:

> Every world-view is conditioned historically and therefore limited and relative. (Dilthey 1959)

> History cannot give a final, universally valid account . . . for the very reason that [aspects of the past] never had a unique and universally valid significance. (Aron 1959)

> All history depends ultimately on its social purpose. (Thompson 2000)

If we pursue these arguments, we will reach an acceptance that anyone's understanding of the past is partial and personal for a variety of reasons. To begin with, the past is in a sense 'unrecoverable' as a whole, with only fragments of it remaining. History is the study of what remains of the past rather than the past itself – what some historians have referred to as the distinction between 'event' and 'fact', the event being what actually happened (which is unknowable in a complete sense) and the facts being what we know of the event, deduced from a range of sources, for example artefacts, documents, witness accounts. So the record of the past is partial. In addition to this, the significance of what remains is itself open to interpretation. Documents will be understood differently by different people. There will be a range of views on how important or otherwise a 'fact' is. Furthermore, there will be a continuum of how 'informed' any individual will be about the context of any historical event, character or site. Given all of this, we can begin to see that we cannot talk in absolutes about 'historical understanding' even amongst those who study history at a relatively advanced level. The understanding an A level student has of, for example, the causes of the First World War will be different to the understanding of their teacher, whose understanding will again be different to that of the professor who may have taught them history at university. Historical understanding is therefore not something you either have or haven't got. It is a process, a continuum that goes from somewhere to somewhere else. The most significant issue of debate for those teaching pupils with special educational needs is probably: where can we say historical understanding begins? What counts as doing history?

If we follow Grove's arguments relating to the way pupils can access literature and apply these to history, then understanding, or experiencing history, like an understanding of literature, can be conceived of as an inclusive rather than an exclusive process. It is one where the beginnings of an understanding of history may be found in the affective responses of pupils, rather than in any knowledge, skills or understanding. In addition to these parallels with Grove's work, the role of imagination in history points to further possible links between a framework for thinking inclusively about history and the one developed by Grove in relation to literature. Historians have always hotly debated the role of imagination in history, but many practitioners have viewed it as central to their understanding and portrayal of the past, for example:

> When we look back on the past, what understanding we gain from it depends primarily on the extent to which we succeed in identifying ourselves with the subjects of our study, thinking and feeling as they thought... (Walsh 1959)

> ...historians are striving to create in their readers the illusion of direct experience, by evoking an atmosphere or setting a scene...It requires imaginative powers and an eye for detail not unlike those of the novelist or poet. (Tosh 1991)

This shows that imagination, emotion, affective responses are a crucial part of the historical process for many professional historians. Without this level of engagement, history is reduced to a hollow chronicle, a list of dates and actions with no human meanings attached. If feeling and sensation are central to an understanding of literature, they are also central to an understanding of the narrative of the past.

To summarise the above, we can begin to develop a picture of 'doing history' as an activity which encompasses the following aspects:

- The personal – the intellectual background of each of us determines the way we 'see' history. We will all have different levels of 'expertise' or understanding. It is arguably only an extension of this argument, rather than a different kind of debate, to argue that pupils with learning difficulties can have a personal understanding of the past even at a sensory level.
- The partial – the past is only knowable in part anyway. If this is taken as a given, then it becomes possible to argue that knowing (sensing) something of the past by, for example, a visit to a medieval abbey ruin by a group of pupils with profound and multiple learning difficulties allows these pupils direct sensory access to that part of history which has survived in the fabric of the building.
- The imagined or sensed – the past is only truly present when we interact with artefacts, stories, buildings, music. It is created by this interplay, and is, as argued above, intensely personal, absolutely partial.

Taking account of the above, and applying Grove's approach, a continuum of access can be developed to be inclusive of all learners regardless of their difficulties if it is said to begin with some kind of apprehension when contact with the past is made in some way. That becomes the starting point for 'doing history' with pupils with special needs.

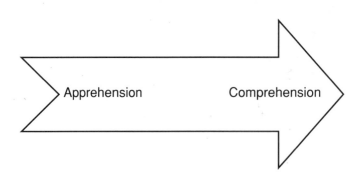

Apprehension of the past can perhaps be illustrated by the feeling we might experience when we walk into an ancient space – an echoing medieval cathedral, a windswept stone circle, a shadow-filled Tudor house. In any of those situations we will apprehend a difference, feel something of what might be called the 'otherness of the past'. History will be sensed. We will feel that the space we are in has a qualitative difference, is apart from our other experiences of the modern world. We will feel some kind of contact with another age. Something of another time will have been sealed into the fabric of the building and into the spaces between.

As informed, literate adults, we will be able play with these feelings in our own imaginations, generate endless possibilities from them. We will be able to live the past in our own ways. Many pupils with special educational needs will not be able to do this, although some will, and the relatively more able pupils who have the title 'SEN' should not be forgotten. For these more able pupils, teachers will be able to give them opportunities to recognise a range of differences between their own lives and the lives of others in the distant past, they will be able to answer some simple questions about an historical site, and may well show some empathetic understanding of what it was like to live in another time through direct experience of what remains of that time.

However, the value for many pupils with significant learning difficulties is not that the experience of visiting historical sites will necessarily lead to the development of any particular skill, knowledge or conceptual understanding. Rather, the experience itself should be seen as valuable for its own sake, for the vicarious contact with another world. However we reach it, the past offers something unique to all of us.

It could also be argued that by allowing pupils to have access to what our society has identified as sites or objects of historical importance we will be providing pupils with part of what Ware (1994) refers to as the uniquely human experiences we should strive to offer all pupils. By allowing them to share in the experiences of exploring historically important locations or artefacts we are

saying something about the way we view our pupils: as people who are part of our history, part of our present.

In practical terms this may well mean that a pupil with profound multiple learning difficulties (PMLD) who visits an ancient building, a church or castle, will make some kind of contact with the past at a sensory level. He or she will experience the space, the light, the shadow, the sounds and perhaps the scents of the place and in doing so will make contact with the otherness of the past, will apprehend a difference, will be 'doing history'.

> A group of Year 1 and 2 pupils are sitting in the remains of a chapel in a medieval abbey. They have walked through stone archways, felt the remains of metre-thick walls and have touched the faces of the stone knights and their ladies worn smooth by the centuries. They made their way to the monks' place of worship where the dark oak ceiling seems to soak up all the light. Now they sit and listen to the sounds of Gregorian Chants being played from a CD. They seem entranced by the music and by the place. Pupils who would not normally sit for more than two or three minutes are still for much longer. Candles are lit and they watch the flames and carry on listening to the music.
>
> It is a magical sight for the teachers. They have no doubt that they have provided something important for their class.

It is perhaps easier to make the case for this kind of direct interaction with history when we are dealing with 'the tangible past' – old objects or buildings which can be seen and touched. But what of other kinds of historical work? Can pupils with PMLD make contact with history which is 'second-hand', perhaps in the form of reconstructions or dramatised stories? Here I think it is useful to shift our conceptions of the way history can be presented, and to see history

essentially as 'story'. The subject becomes a rich source of unique narratives which can be dealt with in the same way as Grove and Park (1996) have worked with literature in their book *Odyssey Now*. Here the otherness of the past is embodied in a set of unique stories which pupils may apprehend or comprehend at a variety of levels. The argument set out above about the use of history to present experiences to pupils which they would not otherwise have had also applies to the use of story. Historical stories are a treasure trove which should be open to all. The practical teaching ideas outlined later in this book will present some examples of how this might be done.

To summarise the argument, however the history we do with our pupils is presented, the central concept is that of the past as 'other'; as something different to the here and now in some shape or form. It is this very difference which makes history a valuable and almost infinitely extendable set of encounters. These encounters can be planned to allow all pupils to gain some access to the otherness of the past. What will change is the way pupils come into contact with that 'otherness', and the kind of things, physically, emotionally and conceptually, they are able to do with this contact.

In this section I have offered reasons for and ways of presenting the history of other people which includes all learners and which is based on the following premises:

- History is an art, and is therefore accessible at a variety of levels.
- The past is a rich source of unique contexts, experiences, stories which are valuable in themselves.
- The past is a universal heritage and contact with this heritage can be seen as one of the experiences which make up our humanity.

Personal history and pupils with special educational needs

The significance of allowing pupils with learning difficulties to have access to their own past as opposed to the more contentious, traditionally defined study of history is something which has long been appreciated in special schools. Even those teachers who may have looked aghast at the idea of teaching something of the Tudors to their group of pupils with severe learning difficulties probably worked happily with them on aspects of their own life stories. But there are still questions to be asked about what we mean by personal past, what forms it might take for different groups of pupils, and how can we make individuals' own stories accessible to them.

For the more able pupils with special needs, the possibilities relating to the teaching of personal histories might include finding out about themselves through photos or video records over a period of time, sequencing personal items, comparing themselves over time, looking at how they have developed as individuals, perhaps through school work, or through their changing leisure interests. It could also usefully include work on their family trees where this is possible and appropriate. If there are issues around family which make such work difficult, then a tree of significant carers or friends could also serve to give pupils a similar sense of themselves as people with relationships which develop and change over time. This work could be presented and developed over time in a variety of formats, including traditional photo albums, illustrated family trees, multimedia presentations, collections of artefacts from holidays, visits and special occasions. If this work was carried on throughout a pupil's school life, they could be helped to build up a record of their life story which was regularly revisited and updated. In this way, they would be helped to maintain and develop a strong sense of themselves as people with a rich and valued past. These techniques and approaches could also be developed for use with pupils with severe learning difficulties, and are already in use in many schools.

The group which perhaps generates the most difficulty for practitioners is pupils with PMLD. It is well-established practice that personal history in terms of routines and sequences are addressed with pupils with PMLD through, for example, objects of reference, photographs, symbols. What may be less explored is their personal past in the sense of past experiences, special events, and family relationships. What should we be doing in these areas?

In developing work on personal histories, the connections we seek to make will be with previously apprehended or comprehended experiences, with memories rather than historical sites or stories. It is important to acknowledge that, in practice, we will probably have no way of being able to verify whether something is being recalled, or if a pupil is effectively experiencing something 'new' to them if there is no memory of the event that is being revisited. If there is no recall, no re-connection, then attempts to develop personal history through, for example, offering pupils some of the objects, sights and sounds they may have experienced on a holiday run the risk of being confusing and perhaps stressful for the pupil who may mistake the objects for cues to an event about to happen in the very near future. Indeed, some may argue that one of the characteristics of an individual with profound learning difficulties is that they exist only in the present, or at most have access to only the very recent past. This may be the case, but I do not think we know enough about the thought processes of such pupils to be certain that a recall of a more distant past is an impossibility.

Ultimately, decisions about the validity of this kind of work will have to be made by those with the most detailed knowledge of the pupils concerned – parents, carers, teachers and support staff. But I would argue that the underlying principle should be an acceptance that personal history is a large part of what makes us human, and we should therefore strive to provide opportunities for every pupil to develop their understanding of themselves as individuals with a unique past as far as that is possible. I provide some examples of how this might be achieved later in the book.

CHAPTER TWO

History teaching in practice – research findings

Romans, swords, horses not cars, me [when I was] little.

Abbey, aged 10, on history

Pupils with moderate learning difficulties

The reasons put forward by practitioners and researchers for teaching history to pupils with moderate learning difficulties were discussed briefly in the first chapter of this book. Most writing about the delivery of history to this group concentrated on the need to look carefully at issues of language and concepts along with the need to use various 'framing' devices to structure and guide pupils' thinking. (See, for example, examples quoted in Sebba 1994.) The use of drama and role-play as a way into effective history teaching for some groups of pupils has also been addressed (see Peter 1994). The main arguments developed in this work could be broadly represented in terms of the need for teachers to make complex, abstract concepts more accessible through simplification, and lively, interactive presentations of strong narratives. While the historical skills of analysis, synthesis, interpretation and questioning were not always explicitly ruled out, most writers tended to concentrate on developing empathetic responses to particular stories and developing pupils' general understanding of significant events and the characteristics of historical periods. Practice in schools, as represented by Ofsted inspections, indicates that a good deal of strong history teaching was taking place with this group of pupils (Ofsted 1999).

Pupils with severe and profound learning difficulties

In contrast to the work on pupils with moderate learning difficulties, there is relatively little published research in the field of pupils with severe or profound learning difficulties and the teaching and learning of history. One of the earliest references is Wilson (1988) who felt that 'History, as the term is generally understood, cannot be taught to these [ESN-S] children' because of their developmental level. This begs several questions, the most significant of which are to do with what constitutes 'doing history' and the link between that and the 'required developmental level' of pupils which I have already discussed.

Wilson's exclusive approach seemed to dominate the 1980s. Throughout this period, there is a significant absence of writing about the teaching of history to pupils with severe and profound learning difficulties. However, the introduction of the National Curriculum, and thereby the subject of history, into special schools changed the landscape. Many teachers were for the first time having to address history as a subject. This no doubt gave impetus to the small number of significant contributions to the debate on the theory and practicalities involved made by, for example, Banes and Sebba 1991, Sebba and Clarke 1991, 1993, Sebba 1994, Ware and Peacey 1993, Turner 1998. These works have concentrated on the ways in which National Curriculum requirements can be made accessible to pupils with severe learning difficulties and also contain some indication of the way in which historical imagination may be developed. There has been limited research on the teaching of personal history, although a notable exception is Banes and Sebba (1991) who looked at ways of making personal history accessible to pupils with severe and profound learning difficulties, some of which are built on in this book.

Overall, the situation is that research into the historical abilities of pupils with learning difficulties in general has been limited, and it has been most lacking with regard to pupils with severe and profound and multiple learning difficulties. This trend continued even after the introduction of the National Curriculum. In part this might be explained by the huge agenda which those involved in special needs had to cope with following the Education Reform Act. Ofsted inspection data indicated that schools were preoccupied with the introduction of the core subjects of the National Curriculum and subjects like history perhaps understandably slipped down the list of schools' priorities (Ofsted 1999). This in turn was reflected in the literature.

Other research

Because of this general dearth of research evidence relating to pupils with learning difficulties it may be useful to look briefly at research into the way young children have responded to various kinds of history teaching. By doing so, I do not wish to imply that the findings of such research are directly transferable to any population of pupils with special needs. I have included it here because it may well give useful insights into how different historical abilities have been developed with younger pupils, and there may be parallels with the kind of work possible with some of the more able pupils with special educational needs.

Young children's abilities in history

Taken overall, the most recent research suggests that the historical abilities of younger children may have been underestimated. There may be some lessons for pupils with MLD in the work that very young children have been shown to be capable of. In one study, Wood and Holden (1995) provide examples of young children's historical thinking at a level which lead them to argue that a

Piagetian 'stage' approach to conceptual development had previously led to 'deficit views of children's potential in this discipline' (p.3). The other examples which follow would seem to support this view. They are presented in chronological order and include examples of work produced in the 1990s relating to the contemporaneous National Curriculum programmes of study.

Knight's 1990 study of Key Stage 1 and 2 pupils led to a cautious claim that 'junior children may understand people distant in culture, place and time' (p.51). The author also challenged assumptions that teaching needs to be based around the immediate environment or real objects. He argues that these assumptions had been based upon a misunderstanding of Piaget's work on the stages of child development. Hodgkinson's 1992 study of 28 Year 5 pupils and 22 Year 6 pupils in two schools showed pupils attaining 'high levels of historical reconstruction and imagination' from primary source materials using what he describes as 'ordinary' teaching by non-specialist teachers. In the following year, Harnett's study of Key Stage 1 and 2 pupils demonstrated that although pupils had some problems in the area of sequencing, they were able to reveal 'a wealth of personal historical information' (p.3) indicating the significance of personal history to children. This is a theme which is developed throughout this book.

In their work published in 1995, Goalen and Hendy argue that drama allowed Key Stage 2 pupils to develop a greater understanding of history than 'traditional approaches', again another theme which has strong echoes in the literature on teaching history to pupils with learning difficulties and one which is pursued in this book. In 1996, Lee et al. published work showing that, although most children could produce historical work of perhaps surprising quality, there were significant variations in the abilities of children with regard to the development of historical skills. They found some seven year olds performing at a higher level than some 14 year olds in some areas of history.

In another work, Wood and Holden's 1997 study of a group of primary aged pupils recorded levels of abilities which paralleled those demonstrated by pupils in earlier studies. The authors found pupils able to demonstrate an understanding of change, chronology and cause and effect through the study of artefacts. They did, however, sound a similar warning to that of Lee et al. when they pointed out that there were likely to be wide variations in individuals' attainments.

In 1998 Hoodless published a collection of small-scale studies of primary aged pupils. Nursery and reception children showed evidence of developing chronological skills, and an awareness of differences and similarities; for example, the differences in uniforms of early policemen and the knowledge that there were no fridges in Victorian times (Hoodless 1998, pp.11–17). Another case study showed that a group of Year 1 pupils were able to sequence events in a story, using chronological vocabulary which included first/before/now/ then/long ago (Hoodless 1998, p.18). The same study also showed that they were capable of reasoning about historical artefacts, comparing similarities and differences and explaining points of view of people in the past (Hoodless, pp.61–3). In another case, Year 2 pupils showed evidence of developing historical understanding and empathy, for example the feelings of a French soldier during the Napoleonic wars (Hoodless, p.94).

Taken together, these works paint a picture of young children, although developing skills at different rates (as might be expected), nevertheless demonstrating levels of historical work which previous, developmentally-based analyses suggested was not possible. This is perhaps encouraging to those of us working with pupils with learning difficulties for two reasons. Firstly, it is another source of evidence which suggests that the way work is presented is vitally important in determining the success of pupils. Secondly, it indicates that the idea that skills and abilities which may have been previously thought beyond pupils with any significant learning difficulty, because *developmentally they would never reach the required 'stage'*, should now be questioned.

This brings us back to the point that we will probably never know what pupils are capable of in history until we offer them a range of opportunities built on a foundation of combined good practice and new thinking.

CHAPTER THREE

Personal history

History is the essence of innumerable biographies.

Carlyle 1838

Literate or illiterate, we are our memories.

Tonkin 1992

This nostalgia of theirs is extraordinary, each of them feels the richness of it. On and on they'll talk; a whole afternoon will disappear while they take turns comparing and repeating their separate and shared memories and shivering with pleasure every time a fresh fragment from the past is unearthed. Living among these old adventures is beautiful, they think...At the edge of every experience is the refracted light of recollection, snagged there like an image in a beveled mirror.

Carol Shields, *The Stone Diaries*

History or memory, or memory *as* history?

In the first chapter of this book, I have argued that it is necessary to re-look at the way we think about history and history teaching. Arguably one of the most significant aspects of history for pupils with learning difficulties (indeed for all of us) is our own biography: the sum total of our past experiences, the path we have taken through life, the events we have taken part in, the feelings these have generated, the imprint left on us. As Shields suggests, the past can be a playground we return to as well as the place where we grew up. Family photographs, videos, the collection of treasured mementos are testament to the human need to record and continually rewrite and retell our own stories, our own history.

School history, to date, has given scant regard to this aspect of the past. This is perhaps surprising given the newly stated core aims of the school curriculum which include 'valuing ourselves, our families and other relationships, the wider groups to which we belong, the diversity in our society...' (DfEE/QCA, 1999a). It is difficult to think of any kind of development in these areas which does not relate in some way to an individual's history. Yet the National Curriculum History Programme of Study contains scant opportunities to develop such links through structured work on personal history. Overwhelmingly, National

Curriculum History has been defined as being about the lives of other people, with only one reference to work on pupils' own lives in one Key Stage. In the Breadth of Study section in Key Stage 1, the document states that pupils should work on 'changes in their own lives and the way of life of their family or others around them.' (DfEE/QCA 1999a, p.104). However, at no other time is personal history referred to in any of the Key Stages.

As discussed in the previous sections, faced with this emphasis on teaching about the past of others, a good deal of imaginative work has been done by practitioners on the ways in which this history could be made accessible to pupils with learning difficulties. However, the issue of personal history has also been one which many teachers have sought to address in various ways. This has led to some degree of redefinition of 'history' within many special schools in order to accommodate personal history work. There is also evidence of a similar approach by inspection teams (Turner 2000) which has tended to support this way of working in many schools.

Evidence suggests that this work has tended to concentrate on the pupils' immediate past in terms of their timetables and recent school events. There is relatively little evidence of consistent work on personal history in terms of biographical developments taking place beneath the umbrella of 'history teaching'. This is not to say such work did not happen – in many schools teaching within Personal and Social Education modules would have included work on 'Myself' which often had a historical or biographical dimension. The fact that teachers felt such work important but did not always feel able to include it in 'history' teaching points up the tension caused by the way the subject has been defined. It seems that many felt something central was missing from the 'official' view of history because of the absence of personal history.

Because of this gap between 'official' and practitioners' perspectives of what should count as history, it may be useful to go beyond the field of education to get another view of what might legitimately be called history. Tonkin, a social anthropologist, has examined this issue and has reached the same conclusion as many teachers of pupils with learning difficulties. She argues for an approach which acknowledges that the personal biography contained in memory is indeed 'history' for that individual. She further contends that any attempt to divide memory and history may not be very helpful as 'in fact one cannot always distinguish their operation' (Tonkin 1992, p.12).

The debate around definitions and boundaries in relation to all of the National Curriculum subjects has been a part of a professional dialogue amongst SEN practitioners since 1988 and was a large part of the review which led to the new QCA Guidance. The issues have been discussed in print by, amongst others, Grove and Peacy (1999) and Byers (1999). Byers (p.184) points out that:

> subject boundaries are uncertain constructs and will remain so. They shift over time . . . [they are] constructs which we impose upon our experiences of the world for our own convenience.'

The new QCA Guidance document for history has apparently embraced this view, and the view of Tonkin, by effectively suggesting a redefinition of what counts as history in its advice that the subject, as delivered to pupils with learning difficulties, should include work on personal memories. In outlining the importance of history to pupils with learning difficulties, the guidance states that studying history offers pupils opportunities to:

Develop an understanding of their personal history alongside understanding about events in the world and what shapes them;

and to learn how:

their own role in their family and community has changed.

This thread goes throughout the Guidance from Key Stage 1 to Key Stage 3. Examples given include, at Key Stage 1, recognising themselves in a video of events that may have happened the same day, placing photographs of themselves in chronological order at Key Stage 2, and by Key Stage 3, recognising themselves and people they know in photos and videos of events which have taken place over a range of time-scales.

Because of these developments, there is now a significant difference in the way history is defined for mainstream pupils and those with special educational needs. The limited opportunity to study their own history afforded to mainstream pupils who will continue to only have personal history addressed in one part of the Key Stage 1 Programme of Study now contrasts with the situation for pupils working below Level 1 of the National Curriculum. For pupils with learning difficulties, the redefinition of what counts as school history will allow their teachers to develop work which will enable them to use their pupils' own past to develop a sense of identity and come to a greater understanding of their own life story. This is something so fundamental that it should arguably be made available to all pupils, regardless of their ability. Not for the first time, it could be argued that the curriculum on offer to pupils with special educational needs may be more pupil-centred and holistic than that offered to others.

Literature relating to life stories

The decision by QCA to include life-history work in the curriculum reflects a growing body of literature on the importance of personal history to the development of our understanding of self and our place in the world. The literature relating to 'life-story' work published in the fields of, for example, cultural studies and oral history offers analyses of the significance of personal history which seem relevant and applicable to pupils with learning difficulties. These frameworks should provide a rich source of ideas and approaches to thinking through the underlying principles of personal history work with this group of pupils.

For example, Paul Thompson, a prominent practitioner and theorist in the field of oral history, outlines the potential significance of the relationship between reminiscence, memory and the self. He describes how work with older people enabled medical staff to discover how 'reflection on the personal past, and through it acceptance of change...might be essential to the maintenance of self-identity' for individuals in their care (Thompson 2000, p.184). Thompson describes how, in the 1960s in the USA, through reminiscence work, older people were enabled to 'reflect upon their lives with the intent of resolving, reorganising and reintegrating what is troubling or preoccupying them' (Butler 1963, p.76). He also outlines an example of similar work in this country in the 1970s – the 'Recall Project' which involved the use of old photographs and music as starting points for discussions with older people living in sheltered accommodation. According to Thompson, the effects were often dramatic:

> In a normal group of rather bored, withdrawn old people, there will be a sudden change of atmosphere...Put simply, people rediscover each other as human beings. (Thompson 2000, pp.186–7)

Similar benefits of such work have been reported by Gibson (1994), again underlining the fundamental human need for access to the past. Thompson outlines how this thinking influenced the growth of similar 'Life Book' work by social workers working with children in care, and also notes how this approach was taken up by workers who supported people with learning difficulties. This approach will be discussed in more detail below.

In an attempt to analyse the broader significance of life story, or biographical history work, Atkinson, R. (1998) has argued that such stories have four classic functions: bringing us more into accord with ourselves, with others, with the mystery of life, and with the universe around us. In short, our own stories are a major part of how we make sense of the world and our place in it, who we are and how we came to be who we are. The significance of personal history as a means of developing a coherent self-identity is stressed by Rosh White (1998) who argues:

> Identity is the name we give to the different ways we are positioned by, and position ourselves in narratives of the past. (p.180)

The development of pupils' self-identity is a central aim for schools and teachers. It is arguably more acute for those who cater for pupils with significant learning difficulties who may not be able to construct their own identities in the same self-contained and self-reflective manner in which most of those without learning difficulties do. We take access to our memories for granted, and arguably only when that access is disrupted do we fully realise the way memories and self are bound together. Work in schools needs to at least consider the ways in which a pupil's history can be presented and represented in order for them to have the opportunity to develop an awareness of self over time and an awareness of self in relation to others over time. The QCA Guidance and, hopefully, this book will provide some starting points for such work.

Life stories and people with learning difficulties

Existing research on life stories of people with learning difficulties has, to date, concentrated on adults. Their abilities to retell personal history has already been demonstrated by the work of Atkinson, D. (1993) and Atkinson, D. *et al.* (1997). The benefits of this work to the individuals concerned has been stressed by many writers, including Gray and Ridden who describe one particular technique of recording personal history, 'lifemapping', a similar approach to the life books referred to by Thompson. This consists of 'a visual representation of "good" or "bad" experiences from birth to the present day... to be used as a point of reference' (Gray and Ridden 1999, p.14). This is described as a process which can 'liberate' people with learning difficulties by challenging stereotypes held by others and allowing participants a role in constructing their own identities through reflecting on their past experiences.

A similar stance is taken by Walmsley (1998), who argues that personal history can be seen in terms of empowerment through understanding:

> Reclaiming that history is important in enabling people to set their lives in a broader context and to comprehend them; it is a step towards empowerment. (p.128)

Although the work referred to above has focused on adults, the principles underlying it are applicable to pupils with a range of learning difficulties. If we argue that access to one's past is a fundamental part of being human, then this must apply equally to all regardless of their abilities. The following examples of pupils with learning difficulties taking part in work on their own history points to some of the possibilities and to the importance of this kind of approach.

Pupils and life history work: some examples

Mathew is a five-year-old pupil attending a special school. He has learning difficulties. He is sitting watching part of the video version of the story 'Granpa' by John Burningham. After the video clip has finished the teacher asks the class about their grandparents. Most of the class have brought photographs of their grandparents. Mathew's hand goes up.

'My grandad is old. He's nice. I like him. He's got old things in his house.'

Later in the lesson, he assembles a family tree using symbols, showing the relationships between grandparents, parents and children.

'My grandad is my mum's dad,' he says. 'She likes him as well.'

Later, Mathew talks to his teacher about how he feels about his grandmother's recent death.

'I miss her. I remember her. She was nice. Gave me sweets when we went round. [I'm] Like the girl [in the video].'

Here, Mathew's sense of belonging to an extended family group is reinforced, as is his understanding of the chronological relationship of his mother and his grandfather. Perhaps the most fundamental issue touched on in this short exchange is that of the way he recalls his grandmother, and his own feelings about her loss. The teacher involved reported that was the first time he had seemed saddened by, or spoken of her death – it seemed that Mathew needed the structure of the lesson to begin to make the emotional connections between a past with his grandmother and the present without her. The session arguably enabled Mathew to begin to reconstruct a self-identity which reflected both sadness at his bereavement and the happy memories he had of his grandmother. There was a clear meeting of learning about a personally significant set of events with the school curriculum.

Amy is a 12 year old with severe learning and physical disabilities. She is using a switch controlled computer programme to look at a 'family album' with a support worker. The album is arranged in two sections, one dealing with her family from grandparents to siblings, and one dealing with Amy's own past from when she was a baby to the current day.

Amy is able to 'turn the pages' to choose which pictures to look at, and to discuss their contents using a mixture of gesture, sign and symbol. For example, she is able to tell her support worker that she was 'happy' when she was on holiday at the seaside, although the weather was 'cold' and 'wet'. She remembers her dad 'falling [in the] sea'.

During this regular session, Amy has demonstrated significant enjoyment of her ability to retell, through a variety of means, anecdotes centred around the people in her photographs. She has made some significant advances in her communicative abilities, has demonstrated good understanding of some sequences relating to her own personal development, being able to identify when she was 'younger', and pick herself out from group photographs taken at different times in her school career.

Once again, there is clear evidence of personally significant events proving to be motivating not only in terms of increasing Amy's understanding of her own place within her family and her own chronological development, but also in terms of her communication skills.

Mark is a 14 year old with profound and multiple learning difficulties. He is working with a member of the school support staff in a quiet area. Mark is presented with a 'time box' which contains a number of items associated with the wedding of his elder sister. Together, the support worker and Mark handle and look at each object; some photographs, one of the decorations from the wedding cake, a silver horseshoe and some of the wedding cards. They later watch a video of part of the reception where Mark and his sister danced together.

> Throughout the session, Mark showed clear signs of recognising many of the people in the photographs and video. He smiled and laughed at the footage of him dancing with his sister, and he clearly communicated a wish to relook at some of the photographs.

This work enabled Mark to revisit an important event in his life. Whatever his level of understanding, he showed pleasure in handling the objects, viewing the images. They clearly held, at some level, significance for him. Put simply, he enjoyed the story they told. They mattered to him.

The introduction of the National Curriculum arguably dramatically challenged and transformed concepts of what relevant knowledge consisted of (see, for example, Mittler 1990, Ashdown *et al.* 1991, Emblem and Conti-Ramsden 1990, Ware 1994), and many special school teachers found themselves coming up against a set of problems Dewey (1956) had identified years previously – the possible conflicts between child and a subject-based curriculum.

> These apparent deviations and differences between child and curriculum might be almost indefinitely widened. But we have here sufficiently fundamental divergences: first, the narrow but personal world of the child against the impersonal but infinitely extended world of space and time; second, the unity, the single wholeheartedness of the child's life, and the specialisations and divisions of the curriculum; third, an abstract principle of logical classification and arrangement, and the practical and emotional bonds of child life.

In the context of history teaching, the National Curriculum introduced its own systems of classifications and arrangements of the past. It framed its own definition of what counted as history in a way which arguably made it more difficult for teachers to deliver the history programme of study and make any connection between the personal world of the child and history subject matter.

The revised QCA stance on what constitutes historical knowledge can be seen as a move towards reducing the deviations and differences Dewey spoke of. What the guidance offers is an opportunity to converge school with the rest of the child's world. What is 'real', what is emotionally charged and significant, what is personal and meaningful is now an accepted part of the History National Curriculum. In this subject at least, there is a new sense of fusion between subject knowledge, or 'school knowledge' and an individual's knowledge of their personal other-than-school world. This may offer renewed hope to those practitioners dealing with pupils with learning difficulties who have sought, over the past decade, to combine subject and individual knowledge.

This is not an argument against the significance and the potential of history as the study of other people's pasts. That is also a valid and valuable entitlement, as I have argued earlier. What the new QCA Guidance does is balance the contribution which wider historical studies can make with the equally significant issues around personal history.

Our own past is now History. That's official.

CHAPTER FOUR

QCA Guidance

The Guidance

Previous sections have referred to the significance of the new QCA curriculum. In this section I will look in more detail at the issues as they relate to history teaching.

In 2001, the first comprehensive guidance on planning and delivering the whole of the National Curriculum to pupils with learning difficulties was published. It seems that, in general, the publication was welcomed by most practitioners, even if many felt it was overdue. The History document sets out the rationale for teaching history to pupils with learning difficulties, and 'Opportunities and activities' at Key Stages 1, 2 and 3. There are two discernible threads that run throughout this document – work on the personal histories of pupils and the opportunity to work on the history of others in more distant times. As I have argued earlier in this book, the acceptance of personal biographies should be seen as a major step for school history teaching. It is one which potentially liberates both pupil and practitioners – pupils can be empowered through a greater self-awareness gained by knowledge of their own past, while teachers are free to work on aspects of history which they have always valued, but the status of which has been unsure.

A similar range of activities related to personal and more distant history work are suggested at Key Stages 1, 2 and 3. However, as history is not compulsory at Key Stage 4, no guidance was produced for pupils at this stage. This book attempts to partly fill that gap in Chapter 5 as I believe that the rationale for teaching history, as outlined in the QCA Guidance, together with the arguments made throughout this book, builds a powerful case for the continued availability of history teaching at Key Stage 4, and at post-16 for those students who remain in the school system.

The significance of personal history and the history of others is outlined in the section entitled 'The importance of history to pupils with learning difficulties' (p.4) and it is worth quoting this section at length:

> Learning history helps pupils develop curiosity in, and an understanding of the past. Pupils learn about the recent past, the more distant past of other people, both famous and ordinary, and how their own role in their family and community has changed.

> In particular, studying history offers pupils with learning difficulties opportunities to

- Develop knowledge and understanding of the sequences, routines and chronological patterns that make up their world
- Develop an understanding of their personal history alongside understanding about events in the world and what shapes them
- Develop knowledge and understanding of how people lived in other times and how those times were different from today
- Experience a range of representations of the past
- Use a range of evidence to find out about the past.

The Guidance goes on to outline suggestions for teaching based upon the thread of developing an understanding of pupils' own histories in the broadest sense, from work on sequences and routines, for example, 'using objects of reference to identify the next activity to be done' (p.8) to more sophisticated work on their own biographies, for example, sequencing photographs of themselves at different ages or 'communicate why they behaved differently at different times of their lives, for example, talking about the changes in what they can do and how the changes were achieved, and what effect these changes have had on the expectations of others' (p.14).

The second thread is based upon a broad range of history work around the history studies contained in the revised National Curriculum 2000 document and linked to the DfEE/QCA schemes of work. An example of this approach is the work linked with DfEE/QCA scheme Key Stage 3 unit 'How hard was life for medieval people in town and country?' Here, pupils are offered a range of opportunities from being able to

> explore some of the sights, sounds and smells of the lives of people in the Middle Ages, for example, through site visits, musical experiences, dramatic reconstructions, cookery, costumes (p.15)

to

> select from a limited range of sources to find out about an aspect of the past, for example, use a textbook or CD-ROM to find pictures that show what life was like in medieval times (p.15)

The Guidance strives to offer a balance between these two threads, but also within each thread there is an acknowledgement of the very wide range of abilities and responses which pupils with SEN will bring to the subject.

Links with other subjects

Throughout the Guidance, links with other subject areas are listed under the examples. Some of the major links are shown below. These links may help practitioners who are involved in cross-curricular planning and who want to link history work with other subjects. (See Figure 4.1)

English	Reporting, recording, listening and story work, poetry, literature, drama and role-play.
ICT	Finding things out, exchanging and sharing information relating to themselves and the past of other people.
Mathematics	Sequences and routines.
Geography	Knowledge and understanding of the history of local places.
Music	Listening to a range of historical music as part of drama, role-play or for its own sake.

Figure 4.1

PSHE and citizenship

History can play a significant part in work on PSHE and Citizenship and there are some clear links to be made between these areas of the curriculum. The Guidance on PSHE and citizenship contains much work which focuses on the development of pupils as individuals and group members. There is clearly a historical or biographical dimension to this work, and there are links to be developed between PSHE/Citizenship and history which can run throughout any scheme developed by schools.

The Guidance for PSHE and Citizenship, in the section outlining the importance and strands of the subject, contains the following references to historical or biographical issues:

1. Pupils can move 'from an immediate time perspective to thinking about the future and reflecting on the past' (p.4), can develop 'a sense of their own identity as a separate and distinct person' (p.5).

In particular, history work can make a contribution to the development of the following knowledge skills and attitudes:

1. Feeling positive; for example by sharing news about their own lives (PSHE and Citizenship, p.8)
2. Reflecting – this offers the opportunity to make links with history work on recent experiences (PHSE and Citizenship, p.8)
3. Developing personal autonomy, for example by using a symbol list to remind them what to bring to school each day. This links directly with history work on routines (PHSE and Citizenship, p.9)
4. Work on 'Developing relationships' (PHSE and Citizenship, p.10) will undoubtedly provide opportunities to develop a historical dimension to this work, while work on 'Sharing experiences' may be done through the sharing of personal histories.

Specific examples of these linkages taken from the PHSE/Citizenship Guidance document include:

1. At Key Stage 1
2. 'develop an awareness of themselves...as individuals...' (PHSE and Citizenship, p.11)
3. At Key Stage 2
4. 'learn about themselves as growing and changing individuals with their own experiences, feelings and needs and as members of their school community...' (PHSE and Citizenship, p.12)
5. At Key Stage 3 in PSE 'they learn to cope with changing relationships' (PHSE and Citizenship, p.17).

History's contribution to other areas of the curriculum

In addition to these subject links, History will provide a valuable context for the development of many of the 'key' and 'thinking' skills outlined in the 'Developing Skills' Guidance document. Some possible examples are given in Figure 4.2.

Performance descriptions

The Guidance also provides teachers with a set of descriptions against which to assess pupils' attainment and progress. These have been written to be as inclusive as possible, with examples of how the earliest levels of attainment, P1–P3, which are common across all subjects, may be interpreted in the context of history teaching. This work has parallels with Brown's suggested continuum of pupil outcomes (Brown 1996). This approach explicitly acknowledges the value of the concept of 'experience' and also provides clear links with cross-curricular learning, for example in the development of communication skills, something argued for by Byers, among others (Byers 1999). From P4 onwards, the descriptors are subject based and are designed to lead into Level 1 of the National Curriculum History Level Descriptors, but still offer the opportunity to acknowledge the use of cross-curricular skills.

Once practitioners begin to use these descriptions, it will become clearer as to how far the Guidance meets the needs of teachers in relation to recording pupil progress and attainment. The example units developed in this book include P Scale information to allow teachers to see how a range of possible pupil outcomes may be related to the 'P numbers'.

Skill	Opportunities in history teaching
Communication	Throughout the subject in a variety of means, from the use of objects of reference to the use of ICT to produce sophisticated presentations and records of pupils' work.
Application of number	Recognising, predicting and interpreting chronological patterns in their own day/week to an understanding of the passage of time over longer periods, the use of mathematical data to look at trends over time, for example the average life expectancy over the past two centuries.
Information technology	The use of ICT to develop cause and effect and therefore the beginnings of some understanding of temporal sequences.
	Investigating sources of historical information, e.g. videos of themselves, CD-ROMs relating to particular historical periods.
	Use of ICT to record their own work and personal development.
Working with others	Guided participation in the exploration of historical sites.
	Developing empathy with historical characters through story, drama, role-play.
	Group work based around a historical theme.
Predicting and anticipating	Predict events based on an understanding of routines.
Remembering	Routines, personal history.

Figure 4.2

CHAPTER FIVE

Key Stage 4 and beyond

That was me. I did that. [I'm] not like that now. Different.

Mark, aged 15

If the arguments about the significance of history as part of a 'cultural entitlement', and perhaps more significantly, as part of the way we develop our self-image are accepted, it is difficult to see how we can justify dropping this kind of work at Key Stage 4, particularly for those pupils who find it difficult or perhaps impossible to spontaneously recall important aspects of their own past. I would argue that schools should offer continuing opportunities for all pupils to reflect on their past, to recall significant events and people as part of their ongoing work. If the value of history as a source of unique stories and experiences is also accepted, then this strand of history also offers valuable opportunities that can enrich the curriculum at Key Stage 4, and beyond.

The inclusion or not of history in the curriculum beyond Key Stage 3 is obviously a decision for individual schools to take. If schools decide not to teach history at Key Stage 4, then the links with Citizenship discussed elsewhere would allow schools to work on personal history, and the examples provided in this book may help with that process. However, it is perhaps worth reiterating the principles identified as underpinning the school curriculum as stated in The National Curriculum Handbook which included:

> valuing ourselves, our families and other relationships, the wider groups to which we belong. (p.10)

As I have tried to show throughout this book, without a historical dimension, a real understanding and therefore a true valuing of self, of others and of community is unlikely to be achieved. If these are things which we treasure, then time should be made available for pupils to explore their history, to make their own links with past selves, with a changing family and developing community. Once again, the central point is the past matters, without it we are adrift, lost in the moment and unable to stand back and say 'this is me, I am made up of those events, relationships and times'. Opportunities to promote this kind of reflection may become even more critical at a time of rapid biological and emotional change and when some pupils will be beginning to think about life beyond school. In times of change, an ability to look back and reflect on previous 'lives', to see the things which alter and those which remain relatively constant may be invaluable.

The study of the past therefore continues to have inherent value, irrespective of the age of the pupil, or the divisions imposed by the structures of the school timetable or curriculum. But these structures matter as well, and they cannot be ignored. Schools may find that additional value can be added to history work by exploring links with accredited courses, for example the ASDAN scheme. Some ASDAN work which could have a significant historical dimension are shown below.

In Transition Challenge, Module 5 on 'Personal Autonomy, 2' a mathematics activity is centred around finding out about special dates and others' birthdays which would provide an opportunity to, for example, look at how individuals have changed over time.

In Module 14, 'Vocational Education', the activity of taking part in Transition Reviews provides an opportunity to do work on the achievements of a pupil over a period of time, how they have changed physically and emotionally, and how their relationships in and outside of school have developed.

ASDAN *Transition Challenge* 2001

In Towards Independence, 'Getting To Know A Group' offers opportunities to use personal history files and records to enable students to 'show that you know who you are', and that they also know something about *where they have come from* in terms of personal development.

In the Module 'Creativity', pupils have the option of producing 'A Book About Me', which would be an ideal opportunity to bring together previous work on personal history in a form which could be accredited.

Similar opportunities exist within the Module on Self Advocacy, where pupils can take part in a project to record their achievements which could involve a review of the way a pupil's skills, abilities and experience have changed over time.

ASDAN *Towards Independence* 1999

Other opportunities for this kind of personal history work exist within the OCR National Skills Profile, for example

---

Skill Area – Personal Skills
Grade – First
Module 4 – Identify friends and family.

Skill Area – Learning Skills
Grade – First
Module 1 – Find out about own strengths.
OCR *National Skills Profile* 1999

These and other areas offer students the scope to develop their understanding of their own past and the way that past relates to their present, and to do so in a way which builds upon previous National Curriculum work. Post-16, this work could also contribute to any package of accredited courses offered by schools.

Possible opportunities and activities at Key Stage 4 and beyond

In the following section I have tried to set out, in a similar pattern to the QCA Guidance, approaches to the teaching and learning of history which may be taken at Key Stage 4, building on previous Key Stages but also recognising the particular issues which emerge for pupils at this age.

Possible progression from Key Stage 3 may be represented as shown in Figure 5.1.

During Key Stage 4 and beyond	
All	pupils continue to develop and extend their understanding of their personal history.
	They take part in work relating to their family history and the history of their locality.
	They experience aspects of the lives of others in the chosen historical periods.
Most	begin to offer simple explanations for why things happened in their own lives and in the lives of others.
	They will select from a range of sources to answer historical questions and to find out about aspects of the past.
Some	will communicate about aspects of their past and about how they have changed over a long period. They will use dates and vocabulary relating to these periods and will make judgements about sources.

Figure 5.1

Ways of working

During the Key Stage, pupils can be taught the knowledge, skills and understanding through opportunities to build on activities introduced in Key Stages 1, 2 and 3, and through work on the following:

The passage of time

Pupils develop and deepen their understanding of sequences and change:

- by the use of video and photographic records of personal celebrations, school and family events to allow pupils to remember and respond to significant events in their past;
- by further extending the use of objects of reference and introducing pictures to allow pupils to recall and predict a sequence of more than one activity related to their changing interests, abilities and activities at Key Stage 4 and beyond;
- by communicating about how they have changed physically and emotionally over their school life, what effect these changes have had on the way they lived their lives in the past and the possibilities for the future;
- by the use of pictures and symbols to identify sequences of events in material in the history of other people and places studied at this stage, for example sequencing the changes which have occurred in the locality of the school over an extended period of time, and by beginning to use vocabulary relating to different periods.

Pupils have continued opportunities for investigating and evaluating the ways of life of different people at different times, and comparing those to their own, for example:

- by actively exploring some of the sights, sounds and smells associated with the lives of people in the distant past covered by the history of other people and places studied at Key Stage 4, through, for example, site visits, musical experiences, dramatic reconstructions;
- by producing, for example, a symbol diary 'day in the life account' for a person who lived in another time and comparing that to their own daily routines. To offer some explanation as to why the people concerned lived in those conditions;
- to choose from a range of sources, which tells us more about an aspect of the past and to use those sources to build up a record of a topic, for example pictures, artefacts, music relating to the period studied;
- to choose from a range of possibly conflicting sources to compile a report on a particular aspect of a period studied, for example, using CD-ROMs, information from textbooks and reproductions of contemporary pictures to assemble a report making some judgements about the sources;
- to further extend their ability to communicate and select from their knowledge and understanding of the past in a variety of ways including the use of dates, vocabulary and conventions that describe historical periods and the passing of time.

This is a very brief indication of the ways in which progression and continuity can be written into any Key Stage 4 scheme of work schools may wish to develop. The examples of units of work which follow in the next section of the book will hopefully provide a more detailed template for possible planning approaches.

CHAPTER SIX

Example units

The past is a foreign country: they do things differently there

L. P. Hartley (1895–1972)

Make the travel arrangements.

What follows is not intended to be a scheme of work. The units will hopefully provide some ideas for the delivery of parts of the history curriculum to a broad range of pupils. They show some ways of working which could be adapted to any period or topic in history. The detailed units could be used as a basis for a set of lesson plans, with modifications for the particular needs of any group. The units are meant to reflect the discussion in the first section of the book, and will hopefully inspire teachers to develop their own creative responses to the challenge of history teaching.

All of the units are based on work developed by the author in a special school catering for a wide range of learning difficulties. Some of the examples have been developed using Microsoft PowerPoint software, digital projectors and the resources of a sensory room. However, similar outcomes could have been achieved in other ways, for example an overhead projector and coloured transparencies could have been used instead of digital images. Sound and music clips inserted into PowerPoint presentations could be delivered by a tape recorder or CD player. The latest technology undoubtedly offers exciting possibilities. However, the quality of any work ultimately depends upon the interactions between teachers and pupils and pupils and their peers. It is up to us to find ways of allowing our pupils to visit the 'other countries' which make up the past.

KEY STAGE 1
A Famous Person – Christopher Columbus
Key Stage 1 OUTLINE

A drama/role-play unit based around the story of Columbus' voyage to the Americas.

Activities	Possible pupil outcomes	P Scales

Preparation of props and materials
 	
For example:
  heavy and light sacks
  metal and wooden bowls
  model ships
  flags
  items of food
	Pupils with PMLD
	Pupils can be assisted in making and/or decorating the various props including silver plates, 'wooden' barrels, model ships. They are encouraged to make choices and communicate likes/dislikes throughout. This can be done as part of integrated art/design and technology work.
		P1–

	Pupils with SLD Can identify pictures of sailing ships, cargo, etc., and make models of these. They can label items with velcroed symbols.	P4
	Pupils with MLD Can locate pictures of items in reference books and use these to make own models, comparing them with modern equivalents.	P7
Drama	Pupils with PMLD Encounter, become aware, respond consistently and become proactive within the context of the drama, communicating choices and responses.	P1–3
	Pupils with SLD Identify items in the drama and respond to the story at various levels.	P4–5
	Pupils with MLD Make distinctions between the past and modern times, follow the story of Columbus.	P6–8
Follow-up work	Pupils with SLD Recognise themselves as participants in the drama from photographs and/or video, recognise items used in the drama and can communicate about parts of the story.	P4–5
	Pupils with MLD Recount aspects of the story and answer questions about the story and associated materials.	P7–8

Figure 6.1

A Famous Person – Christopher Columbus

The story.

For pupils with PMLD/SLD, this would be most effectively delivered over a series of sessions, allowing pupils to develop recognition and anticipation of sequences. For pupils with MLD, it may be more appropriate to deliver the drama in one session and spend more time in developing follow-up work of various kinds.

Activities	Possible pupil outcomes	P Scales
Introductory music Group seated in circle, out of chairs if possible.	Over time, pupils begin to show recognition and anticipation.	
Dim lights *All Chant –* *In fourteen hundred and ninety-two, Columbus sailed the ocean blue...*	Pupils encounter the routine of music, chanting. Pupils join in with vocalisations, Big Macks, use of symbols.	P1(i)–
Teacher – They had to take everything with them on the ship – food, water, ropes, tools. *All – Load the ship!*	All pupils pass items from on to another with appropriate help, e.g. ropes, barrels, sacks. chests, pull items onto ship with ropes, roll up the sail, etc. This can be further extended by offering choice of items to encourage eye-pointing, etc. and asking 'who wants the rope?', 'who wants the sack?' to encourage vocalisation. Pupils with SLD identify items of cargo by matching symbols to objects. Pupils with MLD can later explain the function of some items, e.g. barrels used for storing food and water.	P1(i)– P4 P8
Teacher – Lots of people came to watch them go – and wondered if they would ever see land again or if they might even fall off the edge of the world. *Set Sail!*	All wave goodbye Flags, hats waved Big Macks used to shout farewells	
Teacher – At first things went well. It was peaceful on the sea. They sailed on and on for days and nights. Parachute or large sheet for sail. Unroll the 'sail' and use to make a breeze or use large fan.	Pupils with PMLD are rocked gently side to side. They are given the opportunity to request 'more' throughout. Pupils with SLD/MLD are given jobs to do on the ship – scrubbing the deck, furling the sail.	P1(i)– P3(i)– P4–7

Figure 6.2

Activities	Possible pupil outcomes	P Scales
Teacher – But then the sky began to turn grey. The wind began to blow. Begin to increase wind. **Teacher – The sky went black. A Storm!** Breeze increases. Rain and spray (sprayer). Rocking more vigorous, barrels roll across floor of ship, crew call for help, etc. Roll up the sail. The storm continues. Thunder can be made with a large sheet of hardboard (Rolf Harris style!).	Pupils with PMLD are rocked more vigorously. They are given the opportunity to request more. Pupils with SLD/MLD are encouraged to role-play the parts of crew during a storm.	P1(i)–P3(i) P4–7
Teacher – At last the storm began to pass The wind abates, thunder becomes fainter, then stops. Crew breathe a sigh of relief and began to collect their belongings, and unfurl the sail.		
Teacher – Night fell and the crew settled down to sleep exhausted by the storm. Crew lie down to sleep, use sail as cover. Suitable music.	Pupils with PMLD are covered with blankets/sail. Pupils with SLD/MLD role-play getting ready for sleep.	P1(i)– P4–7
Teacher – In the morning they awoke to a marvellous sight. Use Big Macks to shout 'Land Ahoy!' Cheers from everyone.	Pupils join in with vocalisations, Big Macks, use of symbols.	
Teacher – They paddled ashore. Pupils to paddle in trays of warm water or sand, take time to explore. **Teacher – They thought it was like Paradise.** **They explored the woods and the plants.** Pass around brightly coloured flowers, etc. Some may be scented. **They ate a feast in the sun to celebrate.** Food! This can be pupils' usual snacks, etc., or you could introduce 'New World food', for example pineapples and sweet potatoes.	Pupils with PMLD encounter the experience. Some may react, be able to communicate request for more. Pupils with SLD/MLD role-play the arrival of the crew in the 'New World' and the exploration of the country. They identify props/pictures of trees, river, flowers, etc. The most able later communicate about how they would have felt at the time.	P1– P4 P7–8

Figure 6.2 *continued*

37

Castle Life
Key Stage 1 OUTLINE

A visit to a castle is central to this unit.

Activities and possible outcomes are indicated for the ability range from PMLD to MLD.

Activities	Possible pupil outcomes	P Scales
Look at sources relating to pupils' own homes and then contrast these with a range of sources relating to castles, focusing on what it would have been like to live there, what things were made of and why.	Pupils with PMLD may coactively explore castle sites and drama/role-play experiences. They experience the different textures, the sounds and the feeling of a castle, listen to medieval music and help to make and use a straw pillow or bed.	P1(ii) P2(i)
Photos, video, tape recordings of sounds and photographs of the actual visit can all be used to help to re-create a castle experience in the classroom as well as a stimulus for recognition/recollection work with pupils with SLD (P4). Role-play and to re-enact a day in the life of a castle.	Pupils with SLD will actively explore a castle site and take an active part in drama sessions, using objects appropriately. They may identify some differences between their homes and castles. They may use some symbols related to this work, e.g. castle, stone, old. Pupils with MLD may be able to retell something about the lifestyles of those who lived in castles. They will be able to create their own stories based on their visit and drama work with words and symbols as appropriate.	P3 P4 (P3–4) (P7)

Figure 6.3

Castle Life

Session One – Introduction. What's different about castles compared to our homes?

Activities	Possible pupil outcomes	P Scales
Where do you live? Have a selection of pictures of modern houses (pupils' own homes if possible or a selection from an estate agents).		
Pupils may be given the opportunity to respond to pictures or videos of their own home and family, or an item they associate with home. This will need to be done in a way which does not repeat any 'home-time routine' which may cause confusion.	Pupils with PMLD begin to respond to videos, photographs or items, or communicate the wish to look at particular photos.	P2(i) P2(ii)
Pupils should be given the opportunity to identify which kind of home they live in, or their own home from a choice.	Pupils with SLD recognise themselves in photographs or videos taken at their own home. They may be able to respond to stories about their own home. Pupils with MLD can begin to recount some episodes about events in their own home in the past.	P4 P5 P7–8
All pupils handle a sample of building materials used in modern houses, e.g. brick, slate, wiring, timber. These will be used to contrast with castle materials later in the unit.	Pupils with PMLD encounter these activities. Pupils with SLD are able to identify some objects. Pupils with MLD can communicate about the function of some items.	P1(i)
Make a display with picture of pupil next to the kind of house they live in.		
Introduce idea of castles – big buildings where some people lived in the Middle Ages, 'a long time ago' when life was very different. Set the scene with medieval music. (This will be a common thread throughout the session to allow all pupils to cue into the unit, so the music chosen should be used consistently.)	Pupils with PMLD may operate tape or CD with appropriate switches.	P1(i)–
Show pupil pictures of the kind of instruments used.	Pupils with MLD may be able to identify similarities/differences between medieval and modern instruments.	P7

Figure 6.4

Activities	Possible pupil outcomes	P Scales
Show pictures. Encourage most able to locate pictures in books.	Pupils with PMLD may operate switch activated computer picture-building programmes of castles, continue to listen to medieval music.	P2(i)
Introduce 'medieval family' of children and adults – copied from books, and place them next to picture of castle. Talk about the pictures and point out main features	Explore large stones, feeling weight, texture, coldness.	P1(i)–
	Pupils with SLD to be introduced to selected symbols and to begin to match them to parts of pictures, e.g. castle, tower, wall etc.	P4

For example:
  stone construction
  no electricity
  no glass in the windows
	Pupils with MLD may begin to work out the main differences between their own homes and castles, and begin to talk about what it might have been like to live in a castle.	P7

Have a large picture of a castle on a display board and pupils take it in turns to put the symbol in the correct place.		
Have large stones for pupils to explore.		
Have oil-burning lanterns for pupils to appreciate difference between flame-light and electric light.	All pupils experience medieval music by lamp light.	P1–

Figure 6.4 *continued*

Castle Life

Session Two – The site visit

It may not be possible to visit a castle. However, many old churches date back to the same period and have the same kind of construction. They were built for defensive purposes as well as for worship. They may provide a more accessible alternative which allows pupils to explore an ancient space, look at the construction. If a church is used, then the introductory and site work will need to reflect this.

Activities	Possible pupil outcomes	P Scales
Take as many ways of recording the visit as possible: cameras, digital cameras, video cameras and tape recorders can all be used.		
Cue pupils into the visit with the chosen music and with pictures.	Pupils with PMLD may show some recognition of music used.	P2(ii)
	Pupils with SLD may be able to identify music as 'old'.	P4
	Pupils with MLD may be able to identify music as 'medieval' and communicate about the kind of instruments used.	P7
Pupils with PMLD should be allowed to coactively or independently explore the building and the space. They should be encouraged to touch, listen, vocalise. Their own vocalisations can be recorded – some buildings can give good echoes. Record the sound of the wind through windows or on ramparts if possible.	Pupils with PMLD encounter and react to these activities. They may show interest in their surroundings, and may be proactive in their explorations of the environment.	P1(i) onwards
Pupils with SLD can be allowed to independently explore the site.	Pupils with SLD match symbols or photos to real objects, take photos with adult support, make rubbings of the materials used.	P4
Pupils with MLD carry out structured investigations of aspects of the environment. Allow all pupils to hear the medieval music being played in the castle. Take oil burning lanterns into dark spaces and allow pupils to experience the play of shadow and light.	Pupils with MLD can begin to talk about why the castle was built on the site, what it might have been like to live there. They can use simple maps to find their way round the site, or to record the layout. They can measure the size of walls, doors, windows and fireplaces and talk about what they find. Why were the walls so thick? (defensive) Why are the doors smaller than modern ones? (average height of people was less)	P7-8

Figure 6.5

Castle Life

Sessions Three/Four – The Banquet

This is intended as possible role-play/simulation follow-up work to the site visit and may need to extend over more than one session. The work on recollecting the visit is itself a significant way of developing personal history and adequate time should be given to that.

Activities	Possible pupil outcomes	P Scales
Recollecting the visit All pupils should be given the opportunity to view videos, photos and listen to the sounds recorded.	Some picture building programmes allow the use of own images – some PMLD pupils could switch activate these as well as recorded sounds. Those with SLD can match symbols to parts of the video, recall something about the site, e.g. its size big/small? What it was made of, brick/stone? Have a sample of similar stone for pupils to feel. They can draw simple pictures, or help to create collages of a castle, perhaps using stone-coloured paper cut into appropriately sized sections. Those with MLD can work on detailed pictures or models working from photographs and their own maps.	
Pupils reminded of medieval family – look at their clothes. Copies can be made using material, thick belts, tights, etc. A banquet can be prepared. There are several medieval recipe books available (see Resources section). All pupils can be part of the preparation and cooking of the meal. If possible serve in wooden bowls or on wooden plates. Eat with spoons. Tables can be covered with wood-effect painted sheets to resemble trestles. A log fire can be made from a selection of different types of papers.	Pupils with PMLD encounter, show awareness of, or begin to be proactive in these activities. Pupils with SLD can identify the function of 'medieval' objects and communicate this understanding through sign, symbol or word. Pupils with MLD can communicate about similarities and differences between the life of those living in a castle and their own life throughout the sessions. They answer some questions about castle life.	P1– P4 P7–8

Figure 6.6

Activities	Possible pupil outcomes	P Scales
Lanterns (real or paper) can be hung. The room can be darkened. The banquet is served to the accompaniment of the medieval music used previously. This would be a good opportunity for any member who could juggle to appear as an entertainer. Straw beds and pillows could be made from straw and sacking (watch out for allergies). After the banquet, retire for the night!		

Video this drama and use as a stimulus for further work
 	
For example:
   recognising self in video
   retelling the sequence of events
   as a starting point for imaginative writing/story telling
	Some PMLD pupils can then watch themselves and show some recognition.
	
	Pupils with SLD recognise themselves and can sequence two or more symbols to retell the story.
	
	Pupils with MLD can produce imaginative stories around their experiences.
		P2(ii)
		
		P4
		
		P7–8

Figure 6.6 *continued*

Personal History

Key Stage 1

This unit is in addition to ongoing work on personal history which focuses on patterns, routines and timetables.

The emphasis here is on 'focused recognition or recollection' of significant people, events and objects and relates to the discussion on the importance of history in the development of the concept of 'self'.

Activities	Possible pupil outcomes	P Scales
Pupils are given the opportunity to recognise members of their immediate family or carers, representations of events and objects.	Pupils with PMLD may smile at an item from their home, the sound of a family member on tape, a photograph or video clip of a significant family event.	P2(ii)
They are given the opportunity to recognise significant people and events in their own lives at school.	They may begin to show the ability to predict parts of a video showing, for example, a birthday party, or a school trip.	P3(ii)
Pupils may use Clicker grids to independently or coactively switch-activate family albums containing photographs and perhaps brief recordings of relations' voices.	Pupils with severe learning difficulties recognise themselves and their parents/carers in photos of the recent past, for example, a family celebration. They associate objects and sounds with past events, for example, the sound of the sea, a bucket and spade with a holiday.	P4
Pupils may create simple family 'trees' or personal timelines, focusing on their own development and perhaps their parents' and grandparents'. These trees could include objects, photos and symbols. This should be added to as they progress through school and begin to develop their understanding of family relationships.	Pupils with moderate learning difficulties recognise themselves in pictures of the more distant past and make comments about the events they relate to.	P6–7
The most able can begin to look at sources of information about the lives of their parents and grandparents, for example, through fashion or music.	They understand that they have parents and grandparents, and may begin to understand the chronological relationship between them.	

Figure 6.7

Personal History

Key Stage 1

Time Chests

This may provide a useful way into personal history for pupils with PMLD. However, the note of caution raised in Chapter One needs to be borne in mind. There is a risk of confusion/stress for the pupil if they interpret any of the materials presented as cues to events which are about to happen. Those with the most detailed knowledge of the pupil involved will need to bear this in mind when designing and presenting this kind of work.

Activities	Possible pupil outcomes	P Scales

A time box of a summer holiday.
 	
The box should be individualised and related to its contents by the use of tactile labelling, photographs, perhaps a linked scent to allow it to act as a cue to the contents and work to be done.
 	
The box could contain:
   photographs
   video/sound recordings of family voices
   sound recordings or effects of sea noises – the sea breaking on the shore, seagulls, etc.
   objects might include seaweed, sand, shells
 	
These items can then be introduced by an adult working 1:1 with the pupil.
	Outcomes will hopefully include some degree of recognition/recall by the pupil. This will be very difficult to judge and, as stated above, relies on the detailed knowledge of the pupil developed by staff.
	
	The pupil may begin to show consistent affective responses to the materials, for example, by smiling. The pupil may cooperate with shared exploration of the materials.
	
	The pupil may begin to demonstrate clear choice-making skills relating to the materials.
		P2(ii)
		
		P3(ii)

Figure 6.8

Family History

Key Stage 1

The era investigated will depend on the age of the pupils' grandparents. As with all family history work, sensitivity needs to be shown towards any pupil who, for whatever reason, may have a different family structure. This may mean focusing on the history of parents or carers, rather than grandparents.

Activities	Possible pupil outcomes	P Scales
All pupils will work with photos and videos of their own family to develop recognition. They should have the opportunity to review very recent family events involving grandparents on video wherever possible.	Look for affective responses to sights/sounds/voices. They will experience the artefacts/activities linked to the 1950s (for example).	P1–3
Focusing on a particular generation may help, for example, 'Life in my grandparents' days'. Grandparents' place in family trees – this can be shown via photographs and symbols.	SLD pupils will recognise photos of some of their relatives. They will be able to identify some older versions of items, for example, an old radio, old TV.	P4–5

Pupils with PMLD use Clicker grids or similar to switch-activate 'family books' of relations in chronological order showing grandparents.
 	
Make display of pupils' grandparents.
 	
The 1950s
Investigate a range of sources to identify similarities and differences
Look at:
   televisions/radios
   shops
   schools
   transport
   toys/pastimes
 	
The most able pupils may be able to 'interview' grandparents using tape recorders, talking about any of the topics covered in class.
 	
If possible, invite grandparents into school for afternoon session where pupils organise a tea dance (1950s style) with ration cards, period dress, etc.
 	
Video this for future use.
	MLD pupils will know that they have grandparents, be able to order a simple family tree.
	
	Identify some differences between life in the 1950s and life today.
		P7–8

Figure 6.9

KEY STAGE 2

The Romans

Key Stage 2 OUTLINE

A drama/role-play unit based around the story of Boudicca's revolt against the Romans.

As with the Christopher Columbus unit, this was developed as a Microsoft PowerPoint presentation using scanned images of Roman soldiers and Britons from various sources. It was introduced with the song 'Two Tribes' to give a distinctive identity to the session which can be used to cue pupils in when using the unit over a period of several sessions. Again, a similar effect could be easily achieved by using overhead projector slides to provide the background pictures. The PowerPoint presentation contained a short clip from the film 'Gladiator' (suitably edited) which helped to create a good atmosphere for the battle scene.

Activities	Possible pupil outcomes	P Scales
Preparation of props and materials For example: swords and shields for both Romans and Britons: rectangular and brightly coloured for the Romans, wooden and round for the Britons Roman jewellery armour, clothes laurel crowns for the victorious Romans	Pupils with PMLD Pupils can be assisted in making and/or decorating the various props. They are encouraged to make choices and communicate likes/dislikes throughout. This can be done as part of integrated art/design and technology work. Pupils with SLD Can identify pictures of Roman weapons, jewellery. They can label items with velcroed symbols. Pupils with MLD Can locate pictures of items in reference books and use these to make own models, comparing them with modern equivalents.	P1–3 P4 P7
Drama	Pupils with PMLD Encounter, become aware, respond consistently and become proactive within the context of the drama, communicating choices and responses. They will experience history as 'story'. Pupils with SLD Identify items in the drama and respond to the story at various levels. Pupils with MLD Make distinctions between the past and modern times, follow the main points of the story.	P1–3 P4–5 P6–8
Follow-up work	Pupils with SLD Recognise themselves as participants in the drama from photographs and/or video, recognise items used in the drama and can communicate about parts of the story. Pupils with MLD Recount aspects of the story and answer questions about the story and associated materials.	P4–5 P7–8

Figure 6.10

Boudicca's Revolt

Key Stage 2

Activities	Possible pupil outcomes	P Scales
Introductory music – 'Two Tribes' – Frankie Goes To Hollywood. (A popular group from the 1980s). Group arranged into 'two tribes'.	Over time, all pupils begin to show recognition and anticipation, cued by the music, props, etc. Those pupils with PMLD will experience the drama as a unique story. Pupils may be able to choose which tribe they want to belong to by, for example, eye pointing to appropriate symbols, photographs or actual objects used in the drama.	P2(i)–
Teacher – This is the story of the Romans and the Britons. Two tribes who wanted the same land. **Pupils – We're the Romans. We're the Britons.**	Pupils with PMLD encouraged to contribute via Big Macks or Step-By-Step or similar. Pupils with SLD can identify their 'tribe' by use of appropriate symbols or photographs.	P1–3 P4
Teacher – We're Romans. We have it all. **Pupils – We're the best.** Romans choose items of jewellery to wear, then parade around showing off their finery.	Pupils with PMLD encouraged to contribute via Big Macks. Pupils with SLD sign/use symbols to contribute to the chorus. Pupils with MLD can later explain why Romans would have seen themselves as 'the best'.	P1–3 P4 P7
Britons – We're Britons. We're happy as we are. **Pupils – Happy as we are.**	Pupils with PMLD encouraged to contribute via Big Macks. Pupils with SLD sign/use symbols to contribute to the chorus.	P1–3 P4
Romans – We have to go and fight the Britons. Show them what's what. **Pupils – Show them what's what.** Romans prepare for journey – take off jewellery and put on armour. Say goodbyes.	Pupils with PMLD – as above. Pupils with SLD match and identify items using photos and symbols, dress appropriately with assistance. Later, pupils with MLD can communicate about how they might have felt at leaving families to go to war.	P1–3 P4 P7

Figure 6.11

Activities	Possible pupil outcomes	P Scales
Romans – We're ready. Ready to fight. *Pupils – Ready to fight.* Romans brandish swords and shields. March around.		
Britons – This is our land. It belongs to us. If they come, we'll make a fuss. Ask them nicely to leave things as they are. *Pupils – Leave us alone.* Britons cheer. Gather up their possessions.	Pupils with PMLD – as above. Pupils with SLD match and identify items using photos and symbols. Later, pupils with MLD can communicate about how they might have felt about the Romans.	P1–3 P4 P7
Romans – Times have changed. We make the rules. Romans are in charge now. *Pupils – Romans are in charge.* Romans march up to Britons, grab their possessions. Britons shout 'no!', try to take them back but they're pushed away. Tug of war over items. Romans march off laughing.		
Britons – We've had enough of those thieves. Time to fight back. Take back what's ours. *Pupils – Take back what's ours.* Britons take up their swords. Paint faces – pupils may choose colour for faces by eye pointing, etc.	Throughout these scenes, pupils with PMLD are prompted to contribute to the chorus, and to experience the actions associated with each scene with as much assistance as is required. All pupils will therefore encounter the dramatised story. Over time, this should allow some pupils to develop anticipation, responding consistently to sequences of events and they may become proactive in their interactions, for example, by being able to eye point to their swords when they are needed. They may also begin to communicate intentionally, asking for more of a particular part of the drama. Teaching should allow for this kind of pupil-centred outcome, with preferred actions being repeated.	P1–3

Figure 6.11 *continued*

Activities	Possible pupil outcomes	P Scales
Romans – **We practise fighting all the time** **Not running around screaming** **with painted faces** Romans watch Britons and laugh.	Pupils with SLD may use symbols and words throughout the drama to show recognition of actions and objects. They may be able to predict the next part of the drama and show some empathetic understanding through action, facial expression or words/symbols/signs, for example, by signing 'angry' or 'sad' at appropriate times.	P4–5
	Pupils with MLD – a range of obvious distinctions between their lives and the lives of the Romans and Britons. They show understanding of the events and their sequence.	P6–8
Romans – Try and stop us! **Britons – They're too strong!** The two tribes fight. This can be choreographed as appropriate; for example Romans line up and form a shield wall. Britons hurl 'missiles' (soft balls). Romans then advance, as do the Britons. Two armies fight, then withdraw. Advance/fight/withdraw can be repeated with pupils given control over change of activity by, for example, smiling to indicate 'more' or 'again'. Suitable music can add to the atmosphere, for example, 'The Ride of the Valkyries' by Wagner, or Holst's 'The Planets – Mars: Bringer of War'.		
Britons – The queen is dead. We've **lost it all. Things will never be the** **same.** Britons leave sadly – leave everything behind. Romans cheer, wave swords.		
The victory feast **Teacher – Time to rest – bring on** **the food!** Romans take off armour, put on laurel crowns and drink and eat grapes.	All pupils can share in this end of session feast. This will provide a context for developing communication skills at various levels, and may also provide an opportunity for the more able pupils to recap on the drama.	P7–8

Figure 6.11 *continued*

51

Local history

Key Stage 2 OUTLINE

Activities	Possible pupil outcomes	P Scales
Visit places with contrasting historical content, for example, a church and a shopping precinct.	Pupils with PMLD may coactively explore a variety of sites. They experience the feel, sounds and sights of each site. In follow-up work, they can be presented with records of their visits in various forms.	P1(ii) P2(i)
Record aspects of their visits in a variety of media, for example, audio, video, digital pictures. Look at the lifestyles of the people who built and first used the buildings.	Pupils with SLD and MLD can be assisted in recording aspects of their visits. These can be used in follow-up work, ranging from recollection and identification of sites to the development of multimedia presentations perhaps used as a stimulus for role-play or drama based upon the lives of the people who would have originally lived in the sites visited.	P4–8
Make timelines of the area showing how it has developed over a long period, using a variety of techniques, for example, mosaics, models, two-dimensional tactile wall displays. Art work can be developed in the styles used in the period concerned, for example, 'stained glass' pictures of medieval churches, black and white photographs of Victorian streets, coloured digital images of modern shops. Alternatively, an artefact from each period, or a series of artefacts could be identified and modelled then placed in chronological order to produce a three-dimensional timeline. Local museums are likely to be a rich source of information and activities.	All pupils can contribute to art work, with the most able identifying examples of contemporary art and re-creating that style in their own work.	P1–8

Figure 6.12

KEY STAGE 3/4 OUTLINE UNITS

Key Stage 3/4 OUTLINE

Music and fashion over time – the 1920s to the present. Pupils can work on one decade over a period of time, looking in depth at the lifestyle of the period, perhaps including visits to museums if locally available. Alternatively, they may work on more than one decade for consecutive single sessions, giving a contrast between clothes and music.

Activities	Possible pupil outcomes	P Scales
Arrange – Pupils to explore representations of fashion (reproduction or original, depending on the age of your colleagues) and to listen to music from the periods concerned.	PMLD pupils will experience a range of music and dance routines and demonstrate a preference. They will control recordings of music with switches.	P1–2(ii)
A fashion parade/day based around one of the decades. Combine this with a dance/disco with appropriate music, clothes, food, drinks.	SLD pupils will identify some differences in the styles of music and dress, etc. They will express preferences and be able to match styles of dress with the styles of music.	P5
For example: a 1940s' tea dance a 1950s' rock and roll session a 1960s' 'peace and love' concert a 1970s' disco.	MLD pupils will be able to match activities and music with periods of time and talk about the periods concerned.	P7, P8

Figure 6.13

Key Stage 3/4 OUTLINE

Britain since 1930 – the home front in the Second World War.

Activities	Possible pupil outcomes	P Scales
Pupils will experience a range of activities based upon life in the Second World War. These could include:		
'Digging for Victory' – the planting and tending of a vegetable allotment, with the use of wartime recipes to create a 'war tea party' complete with contemporary music and dress.	Pupils with PMLD will encounter the activities and experiences and may engage in coactive exploration of the sights, sounds, tastes and smells of the activities. Some may be able to make choices within the sessions.	P1(i)–3
Drama based around a child's view of the Blitz. This might include: air raid sounds, bombers flying overhead, hiding in a shelter, listening to the bombs fall, emerging from the shelter to see the destruction caused by the bombing.	Pupils with SLD recognise the function of everyday objects from the 1940s. They may recognise some distinctions between the past and the present and say how they feel about the experiences in the drama.	P4–6
A visit to a steam train line may be possible – many have wartime themed days (or might be persuaded to host one) where pupils could experience the atmosphere, perhaps of an evacuation.	Pupils with MLD will be able to recall and predict important elements of the drama/role-play and recognise distinctions between the lives of those living in the 1940s and their own lives.	P7–8
Similarly, some working farm museums may be able to provide special 1940s visits to enable pupils to look at the lives of those who worked on the land in this period.		

Figure 6.14

Key Stage 3/4 OUTLINE

The Blitz – A drama/role-play session based upon the bombing of London.

Activities	Possible pupil outcomes	P Scales
Introductory music – 1940s' singer, perhaps Vera Lynn singing 'We'll meet again'. Group seated around a table for a 1940s' teatime in a kitchen. Props include a tape recorder disguised as a 1940s' radio, gas masks.	Over time, all pupils begin to show recognition and anticipation, cued by the music, props, etc. Those pupils with PMLD will experience the drama as a unique story.	P2(i)–
Pupils pass round bread and butter. A siren begins to wail. The music is stopped. All sit and listen. Teacher – 'Listen'. 'Listen' repeated as a chorus. Pupils join in with Big Macks or similar. They collect their gas masks, wearing them if appropriate.	Throughout these scenes, pupils with PMLD are prompted to contribute to the chorus, and to experience the actions associated with each scene with as much assistance as is required. All pupils will therefore encounter the dramatised story. Over time, this should allow some pupils to develop anticipation, responding consistently to sequences of events and they may become proactive in their interactions, for example, by being able to eye point to their gas masks. They may also begin to communicate intentionally, asking for more of a particular part of the drama. Teaching should allow for this kind of pupil-centred outcome, with preferred actions being repeated.	P1–3
	Pupils with SLD may use symbols and words throughout the drama to show recognition of actions and objects. They may be able to predict the next part of the drama and show some empathetic understanding through action, facial expression or words/symbols/signs, for example by signing 'frightened' at appropriate times.	P4–6
	Pupils with MLD a range of obvious distinctions between their lives and the lives of those who lived through the Blitz. They show understanding of the events and their sequence.	P7–8

Figure 6.15

55

Activities	Possible pupil outcomes	P Scales
Teacher – Go quietly to the shelters. Pupils are 'led' to a shelter. This could be a rearranged classroom or another part of the school, perhaps a sensory room. The shelter is dark, only lit by torches or similar.	As above	
Teacher – Put that light out! Dark, dark, dark – staff and pupils chant quietly. Music could be used to add to the tension – perhaps 'Mars' from Holtz's 'The Planets Suite'. Pupils sit in the dark – hold hands and sway gently. **Teacher – The bombers are coming.** The sound of aircraft can be heard gradually getting louder. **They're coming!** – repeat as a whisper then getting louder, build up expectations.		
Bombs! Loud sound of bombs falling/exploding. Flashes of light can be seen (red-coloured lights can be flashed on and off). **They've gone, we're safe.** Repeat as before, building from whisper to loud shouts of relief. The sound of planes getting fainter. Pupils slowly gather themselves together to return to their kitchen.		
Oh no! They return to a kitchen where the furniture is upturned, smell of smoke (if possible). The 'radio' is playing 'We'll meet again'. Staff and pupils put the kitchen back together, sit down again at the table and continue their meal.	This will provide a context for developing communication skills at various levels, and may also provide an opportunity for the more able pupils to recap on the drama, discuss their feelings and the feelings of those who lived through the times.	

Figure 6.15 *continued*

Personal history

Key Stage 3/4 OUTLINE

Activities	Possible pupil outcomes	P Scales
Pupils to revisit a wide range of personal history based on events in their family and at school using photographs, video recordings, tapes, oral recollections, pieces of work. Pupils with PMLD are offered opportunities to explore/experience History Chests of personal artefacts relating to significant events. It could be used as a means of marking an important transition in their lives – from school to post-16 provision of whatever kind.	Pupils with PMLD encounter their past through the use of 'Time Chests' as in previous Key Stages. They may use Clicker grids to switch-activate 'family books' of relations and activity/achievement books in chronological order spanning a period of time.	P1(i)– P2(ii)–
	SLD pupils recognise a range of familiar people and themselves in pictures of the past. They match symbols to pictures of their own family. They recall activities and events which they have taken part in throughout their school life.	P5
	MLD pupils can recount episodes from their past with minimal prompts and can comment on why things happened in a particular way, and how things might have changed if they had behaved differently. They review their successes and experiences over their school life, discussing likes and dislikes and begin to use these as part of their decision-making relating to their future.	P7–8

Figure 6.16

Remembrance Day – An Assembly

Key Stage 3/4

Historical anniversaries provide excellent material for short, focused sessions and could be used as material for a whole school assembly. Remembrance Day could be marked in this way.

Activities	Possible pupil outcomes	P Scales
Pupils enter room/hall that has been darkened. Candles are burning in a row at the front of the hall. Teacher introduces the session. ***Today we're going to remember those who died in wars.*** A video clip is played – an extract from the TV series 'Band of Brothers', showing a single soldier running. The soldier aims his rifle and shoots. The picture is paused. One by one the candles are snuffed out. The teacher reads a poem, perhaps from Brian Gardner 1977, 'The Terrible Rain. The War Poets 1939–1945' (London, Methuen). This can be symbolised and displayed on an overhead projector. While the poem is being read, poppies are passed around. A wartime song is played, perhaps from a compilation of 1940s' popular songs. A video of the Cenotaph is played. Pupils listen to 'The Last Post'. The teacher begins to light the candles. ***We say thank you to those who died so that we could be safe.*** The lights are put back on and pupils leave the hall while quiet, reflective music is played. Pupils can place their poppies at the front of the hall. Previous art work could have produced a large statue of a soldier, perhaps made of wire covered with plaster soaked material and spray painted silver or bronze. The poppies could be laid at the base of the statue. In follow-up work – Most pupils may be able to produce work focusing on the feelings of the soldiers and their relatives. They may visit war memorials. Some may be able to compose their own poems or stories about loss and war.	All pupils encounter the atmosphere of the room. They may show awareness of the change in light, or of the candles. They encounter and may react to the changes of sound, light and mood throughout the session. They may cooperate with exploring, holding and releasing their poppies and may be able to locate the candles and the video. Most pupils will recognise the session as being about soldiers and wars. They may recognise the poppies and be able to say where they have seen them before. They may be able to communicate about the way the music, pictures and poetry made them feel. Some pupils will be able to recognise the poppy as a symbol of Remembrance Day. In follow-up work – Most may know that people get killed in wars. They may be able to identify loss as sad for those involved. They experience the atmosphere of a war memorial. Some will be able to talk about their own feelings about the session and be able to write, draw or talk about how they might have felt if they were a soldier, or the relative of a soldier who died in a war.	P1(i)– P4 P7 P4–5 P7–8

Figure 6.17

Summary and conclusions

I have tried to argue for a view of history and history teaching which is inclusive of all pupils. I have argued that history can be seen as an art, and as such can be experienced and understood at a variety of levels. All of us will have met the past at a variety of levels. Our own experiences of history may include an encounter with a historical site about which we know very little, yet in which we feel a sense of a past time, glimpse the possibilities of other lives. Our experiences may also include detailed knowledge and understanding of the story of a particular event or period in time, either personal or of the lives of those who lived in the distant past. Both kinds of history add something to our enjoyment and understanding of the world and to our knowledge and understanding of ourselves as creatures who exist in time and through time. This continuum of contact with the otherness of the past is something we can and should offer to pupils.

I have argued that history should be made available to all because:

- The past is a rich source of unique contexts and stories which are valuable as experiences in themselves. It is a source of narratives so diverse, often so fantastic and always so fascinating that not to include a selection of these tales in all pupils' educational diets is surely to do a disservice to those pupils. History matters as story, because stories matter. To all of us.

- The past is a universal heritage and contact with this heritage can be seen as one of the experiences which make up our humanity. If we see education in terms of sharing and disseminating the things society values, then we must make the effort to share the past with our pupils. We teach history because history matters, has a value of its own. To ignore history would be to ignore a large part of what makes us human.

- The development of self-identity is a major part of the work of schools. Personal history is a major part of self-knowledge. By presenting all pupils with opportunities to encounter, interact with and develop their own stories they will learn to see themselves as individuals with a valuable past as well as an important present and future. The personal past of all our pupils is part of 'doing history'.

- History can also be a personal playground. It is a source of wonderful recreation as well as re-creation. All of us will have sat with our photographs, our mementos, our memories and enjoyed the pleasure of the past, revelled in the telling and retelling of our lives. This is history as sheer pleasure. Again, we should work to ensure that none of our pupils miss out on this necessary luxury.

All of these aspects of history are now firmly on the agenda for pupils with learning difficulties. Many schools, many practitioners will have spent years developing their own approaches to the teaching of history that acknowledged some if not all of the above. But until recently, the official guidance offered by various agencies has been, at least in part, out of step with what many saw as the needs of their pupils. The new QCA Guidance on the planning and delivery of the history curriculum arguably marks a watershed in terms of the way history in schools can be defined. History can be inclusive, can be broadly based and yet also deeply personal. Pupils can be offered the best of all historical worlds. I hope that this book goes some way to helping practitioners deliver this new entitlement. This book is rooted in the belief that history is crucial to us all, in a myriad of ways. We exist in the place where the past and future meet. Being able to look back means we can be more certain of ourselves and our place in the world, and can enjoy the telling of stories about what has gone before.

Resources

I have tried to give a flavour of the kind of resources which could be used to develop materials, or to support visits. I have not tried to list those books, picture packs, etc., produced by educational publishers as these are well known or information on them is easily obtainable. The Internet is a rich resource for teachers of history and I have tried to indicate the range of sites which may be useful. Any such list, however, is unlikely to meet individual needs. Using a search engine to locate specific resources is highly recommended.

As previously stated, many of the examples of teaching materials used in this book were created using Microsoft PowerPoint software, and delivered using a digital projector. Given the increased use of this kind of technology in most schools, this seems to be a realistic and potentially exciting way forward for history teaching. Such an approach offers teachers the opportunity to make their own interactive resources based on their own needs, and could be the basis for shared development work involving a number of schools. Because of this, many of the resources suggested below can be used in this way. However, for those schools not able to make use of this technology a very similar effect could be achieved using overhead projectors and printed acetates containing appropriate images, alongside tapes or CDs of sound effects or period music.

General Internet sites

www.inclusivehistory.info
This is the author's own web site which will hopefully be a useful on-line history resource for teachers of pupils with learning difficulties. My aim is to include examples of good practice, teaching resources in various formats as well as links to other sites.

www.historybookshop.com
A good potential source of teacher resources, for example, period cookbooks.

www. history.org.uk
The site of The Historical Association which publishes, amongst other things, *Primary History* which contains practical ideas for teaching history which may be adapted for pupils with special needs.

www.bbc.co.uk
This site contains excellent historical material and a wide range of links.

www.historyonthenet.co.uk/

www.schoolshistory.org.uk/
Both of the above contain useful links and material which may be adaptable.

General photographs and images

There is a multitude of free images available on the web, but tracking down what you want can be time consuming. A good scanner to use images from books is well worth the investment. Copyright law needs to be observed. There are many collections of images available on CD-ROMs; again sifting through material can take some time, but these images are usually copyright-free.

Historic postcards can provide excellent pictorial resources.

Web sites containing useful images/photographs.

www.imagesofengland.org.uk

www.freeimages.co.uk
This site contains general images which could be useful in developing PowerPoint or similar resources. Similar sites can be found using any good search engine.

Many towns and villages have web sites which contain good local information and many have old photographs – try searching under the name of a local town.

There are also many published books containing photographs of national and local events and these can often be found in 'bargain book shops' at very good prices.

Re-enactment societies

There are a huge number of societies which specialise in re-creating periods of history. Many will offer a service to schools, and could be used to provide a focus for project work, drama, etc. Examples are listed below.

www.vikings.ndirect.co.uk

www.the-reenactor.co.uk/

www.sealedknot.org/

Artefacts

Sets of replica artefacts are sold through most educational catalogues and museums will often lend boxes of artefacts relating to particular periods.

Museums

Local museums are likely to be excellent sources of information and inspiration. A comprehensive list of museums can be found at

www.mda.org.uk/vlmp/

Music

Period music can be an excellent way of setting a scene, contributing to atmospheric drama or role-play or to use to accompany a site visit. Collections of music from most periods are now easily available on CD, for example the HMV 'Easy' series which includes 'Songs of World War II collection', and the '1930s Classics collection'. Music from the Middle Ages and the Rennaisance is also available on a number of record labels.

The BBC has a good selection of musical clips from different ages at

www.bbc.co.uk/music/timeline

Videos/television series

Local video compilations may be available for your own area. Videos containing archive footage of events from almost all decades of the twentieth century are available, for example the 'A Year To Remember' series which is stocked by most large video stores and is available on-line from bookstores such as Amazon.com.

Other possible resources include 'The World At War' and Simon Schama's 'A History of Britain'. These include either archive footage or reconstructions of events.

Many historical dramas can also provide short clips of film which can be used in PowerPoint presentations, or as a stimulus on their own. Most will need to be carefully edited. Examples include:

Shakespearean adaptations, for example Henry V. Good on period costume, some fight scenes and a general flavour of the period.

Gladiator – a wonderful re-creation of a battle scene near the beginning of the film.

Band of Brothers – some realistic footage which could be used with care.

There have been a large number of history programmes in recent years which have included excellent re-creations of various periods. It may be worth looking at The History Channel as another potential source of video footage. Their broadcast schedules are published on their web site

www.thehistorychannel.co.uk
which also contains links to other internet sites.

Historical sites

Local knowledge is essential here – talk to your local museum staff if you're not sure about what's on offer. For trips further afield, the following may help:

Steam railways

These offer an excellent opportunity for pupils to experience a range of role-play or similar activities. The site below provides a comprehensive list of historic railways open to the public. Many will provide specialist educational activities.

www.railcentre.co.uk/railuk/mainuk.htm

Castles are always popular and motivating; for information see

www.english-heritage.org.uk

www.nationaltrust.org/

References

Aron, R. (1959) 'Relativism in History', in Meyerhoff, H. (ed.) *The Philosophy of History in Our Time*. New York: Doubleday Anchor Books.

ASDAN (1999) *Towards Independence*. Bristol: ASDAN

ASDAN (2001) *Transition Challenge*. Bristol: ASDAN.

Ashdown, R., Carpenter, B. and Bovair, K. (1991) 'The curriculum challenge', in Ashdown, R., Carpenter, B. and Bovair, K. (eds) *The Curriculum Challenge: Access to the National Curriculum for Pupils with Learning Difficulties*. London: Falmer Press.

Atkinson, D. (ed.) (1993) *Past Times: Older People with Learning Difficulties Look Back on Their Lives*. Buckingham: Open University Press.

Atkinson, D., Jackson, M. and Walmsley, J. (1997) *Forgotten Lives*. Kidderminster: BILD Publications.

Atkinson, R. (1998) *The Life Story Interview*. London: Sage.

Banes, D. and Sebba, J. (1991) 'I was little then: accessing history for pupils with severe learning difficulties', *British Journal of Special Education* **18**(3), 121–4.

Birt, D. (1976) 'All-ability history', *Teaching History* **4**(16), 309–25.

Brown, E. (1996) *Religious Education for All*. London: David Fulton Publishers.

Butler, R. (1963) 'The life review: an interpretation of reminiscence in the aged', *Psychiatry* (**26**), 65–76.

Byers, R. (1999) 'Experience and achievement: initiatives in curriculum development for pupils with severe and profound and multiple learning difficulties', *British Journal of Special Education* **26**(4), 184–8.

Carpenter, B., Ashdown, R. and Bovair, K. (eds) (1996) *Enabling Access: Effective Teaching and Learning for Pupils with Learning Difficulties*. London: David Fulton Publishers.

Cowie, E. E. (1979) *History and the Slow-learning Child: A Practical Approach*. London: Historical Association Pamphlet 41.

Dewey, J. (1956) *The Child and the Curriculum: The School and Society*. London: University of Chicago Press.

DfEE/QCA (1999a) *The National Curriculum. Handbook for Primary Teachers in England*.

DfEE/QCA (1999b) *The National Curriculum. Handbook for Secondary Teachers in England*.

Dilthey, W. (1959) 'The dream', in Meyerhoff, H. (ed.) *The Philosophy of History in Our Time*. New York: Doubleday Anchor Books.

Emblem, B. and Conti-Ramsden, G. (1990) 'Towards Level 1: reality or illusion', *British Journal of Special Education* **17**(3), 88–90.

Galletley, I. (1981) 'For humanities' sake', *Special Education, Forward Trends*, **8**(1), 25–6.

Gibson, F. (1994) *Reminiscence and Recall: A Guide To Good Practice*. London: Age Concern England.

Goalen, P. and Hendy, L. (1995) '"It's not just fun, it works!" Developing children's historical thinking through drama', *The Curriculum Journal* **4**(3), 363–84.

Gray, B. and Ridden, G. (1999) *Lifemaps of People with Learning Disabilities*. London: Jessica Kingsley Publishers.

Grove, N. (1998) *Literature For All*. London: David Fulton Publishers.

Grove, N. and Park, K. (1996) *Odyssey Now*. London: Jessica Kingsley Publishers.

Grove, N. and Peacey, N. (1999) 'Teaching subjects to pupils with profound and multiple learning difficulties', *British Journal of Special Education* **26**(2), 83–6.

Harnett, P. (1993) 'Identifying progression in children's understanding: the use of visual materials to assess primary school children's learning in history', *Cambridge Journal of Education* **23**(2).

Hodgkinson, K. (1992) 'Young children's ability to integrate historical data from primary sources', *Research in Education* **48**, 85–91.

Hoodless, P. (ed.) (1998) *History and English in the Primary School: Exploiting the Links*. London: Routledge.

Knight, P. (1990) 'A study of teaching and children's understanding of people in the past', *Research in Education* **44**, 39–53.

Lee, P., Dickinson, A. and Ashby, R. (1996) 'There were no facts in those days: children's ideas about historical explanation', in Hughes, M. (ed.) *Teaching and Learning in Changing Times*. Oxford: Blackwell.

Martin, C. and Gummett, B. (1996) 'History' in Carpenter, B., Ashdown, R. and Bovair, K. (eds) *Enabling Access: Effective Teaching and Learning for Pupils with Learning Difficulties* (2nd edn, 2001). London: David Fulton Publishers.

Mittler, P. (1990) 'Foreword', in Fagg, S., Aherne, P., Skelton, S. and Thornber, A. *Entitlement for All in Practice: A Broad, Balanced and Relevant Curriculum for Pupils with Severe and Complex Learning Difficulties in the 1990s*. London: David Fulton Publishers.

Ofsted (1999) *Special Education 1994–1998. A Review Of Special Schools, Secure Units and Pupil Referral Units In England*. London: HMSO.

Oxford, Cambridge and RSA Examinations (1999) *National Skills Profile Handbook*. Cambridge: Oxford, Cambridge and RSA Examinations.

Park, K. (1998) 'Dickens for all: inclusive approaches to literature and communication with people with severe and profound learning disabilities', *British Journal of Special Education* **25**(3), 114–18.

Peter, M. (1994) 'History through drama', in Sebba, J. *History for All*. London: David Fulton Publishers.

Roberts, M. (1972) 'History – a waste of time?', *Special Education* **61**(4), 19.

Rosh White, N. (1998) 'Marking absences: Holocaust testimony and history', in Pers, R. and Thomas, A. (eds) *The Oral History Reader*. London: Routledge.

Sebba, J. (1994) *History for All*. London: David Fulton Publishers.

Sebba, J. (1995) 'History for pupils who experience severe difficulties in learning', in Potts, P., Armstrong, F. and Masterton, M. (eds) *Equality and Diversity in Education: Learning, Teaching and Managing in Schools*. London: Routledge.

Sebba, J. and Clarke, J. (1991) 'Meeting the needs of pupils within History and Geography', in Ashdown, R., Carpenter, B. and Bovair, K. (eds) *The Curriculum Challenge: Access to the National Curriculum for Pupils with Learning Difficulties*. Lewes: Falmer Press.

Sebba, J. and Clarke, J. (1993) 'A response to "We're doing history"', *British Journal of Special Education* **20**(4), 141–2.

Shields, C. (1993) *The Stone Diaries*. London: Fourth Estate.

Thompson, P. (2000) *The Voice of the Past. Oral History*, 3rd edn. Oxford: Oxford University Press.

Tonkin, E. (1992) 'Narrating our pasts: the social construction of oral history', *Cambridge Studies in Oral and Literate Culture 22*. Cambridge: Cambridge University Press.

Tosh, J. (1991) *The Pursuit of History: Aims, Methods and new directions in the study of modern history*, 2nd edn. London: Longman.

Turner, A. (1998) '"It would have been bad": the development of historical imagination and empathy in a group of secondary aged pupils with severe learning difficulties', *British Journal of Special Education*, **25**(4), 164–7.

Turner, A. (2000) 'Redefining the past: Ofsted, SLD schools and the teaching of history', *British Journal of Special Education* **27**(2), 67–71.

Walmsley, J. (1998) 'Life history interviews with people with learning disabilities', in Pers, R. and Thomas, A. (eds) *The Oral History Reader*. London: Routledge.

Walsh, W. H. (1959) 'Can history be objective?', in Meyerhoff, H. (ed.) *The Philosophy of History in Our Time*. New York: Doubleday Anchor Books.

Ware, J. (1994) 'Implementing the 1988 Act with pupils with PMLDs', in Ware, J. (ed.) *Educating Children with Profound and Multiple Learning Difficulties*. London: David Fulton Publishers.

Ware, J. and Peacey, N. (1993) '"We're Doing History" – What does it mean?', *British Journal of Special Education* **20**(2), 65–9.

Wilson, M. D. (1988) *History for Pupils with Learning Difficulties.* London: Hodder and Stoughton.

Wood, L. and Holden, C. (1995) *Teaching Early Years History.* Cambridge: Chris Kingston Publishing.

Wood, E. and Holden, C. (1997) '"I can't remember doing Romans" – the development of children's understanding in history', *Teaching History* **89**.

Zeldin, T. (1995) *An Intimate History of Humanity.* London: Minerva Paperbacks.

Index